Eat your Com for Lunch!

27 Golden Rules of running a successful and profitable food business – and enjoy doing it!

By Ali Carter

How this book will help you

Introduction

This book will make you more money.

It will show you how you can easily squeeze more profit per dish out of your commercial kitchen without damaging your customer offer.

In fact, I'll show you how you can improve your offer, increase sales and enlarge your gross and net profit margins.

Bold claims? Yes. But I've done all these in many hospitality outlets and now I'm sharing the secret with you.

Let's kick-off with some killer facts: the UK hospitality sector serves 20,000,000 meals every week. Now, if each of those twenty million weekly meals was just 5p more profitable, not with a customer-scaring price hike but through additional profit easily generated through better portion control, improved menu design, less waste, better buying practices, better customer understanding and better kitchen management, that would be another £1,000,000 a week in the pockets of hospitality business owners. I'm sure you'd like your share of that extra £1m!

And the great news is: if you follow my rules, you could well achieve more than that easy 5p increased margin per dish. Substantially more. But for the moment we'll stick to the modest 5p figure.

It really is very simple: the extra cash is there for the taking. To search and find these 5ps takes an eye for detail and a will to implement discipline and structure to the production and service of great food.

Ashley Palmer-Watts who heads up Dinner, part of Heston Blumenthal's group of restaurants, sums this up nicely: 'If a recipe says 27 grams of flour, it's 27 grams, not 29 or 26, there's no guesswork, it's about precision.' One of the reasons Heston has become so successful lies within this philosophy.

Whether you run a humble sandwich shop or have aspirations to be the next big food franchise operation, there are 27 Golden Rules to achieving success. Follow these steps and you will avoid all the disasters inexperienced operators make.

Who this book is for

This book is for anyone cooking and serving food - whether just starting out or established but not thriving. Someone who wants a blueprint to fast-track them to a profitable and sustainable business. And also to enjoy doing it – it's important that you wake up each morning wanting to get to work – and you'll only achieve that if you're profitable and staff and customers respect your professionalism.

Is this you?

You have a 'thunderbolt' moment: 'I want to run my own pub, restaurant, hotel, sandwich shop, café'.

You have always had a passion for exciting food – you know you could do so much better than all those cafes and restaurants you see doing OK with mediocre or even poor food and service. After all, how hard can it be to knock up a bit of grub, serve a few drinks and keep a genial conversation going with the customers?

If you're thinking: 'How hard can it be?' or 'What could possibly go wrong?' This book's for you.

You're just leaving the safe world of the employed for the freedom (or as you may find, the gut-wrenching, bank account-draining terror) of running your own hospitality business – a top notch restaurant, pub grub or organic café - it's going to be the best thing ever.

You're in charge. This is your dream. To finally run your own business. Your mind races through the endless opportunities. Your new-found freedom is intoxicating! Your restaurant/café/pub/food business is just about to take off and you're in the driving seat.

If your mind is running away with you and the scale of the task ahead seems daunting - and you want to know where to start - this book's for you.

If just one of the following questions strikes a chord with you, you need this book. You're already running a food business and wondering why you're not living the dream. Is this you?

1. You can remember the day you started: the passion for food; the aim to create a successful business doing what you love - but it hasn't turned out like you thought

2. There's never any cash left after the bills are settled and you can't pinpoint why

3. Life's business decisions are happening to you - not made by you

4. Your chef and staff rule the roost and you can't seem to control them

5. Your exquisitely furnished restaurant sits empty of customers while the café down the road is packing them in and you don't know why

6. Your mind is puzzled as to why the dream is turning sour

If the answer is yes, then this book's for you.

You're a chef who cooks amazing food but finds the detail of being responsible for the entire business a challenge.

As a chef the day-to-day task of sourcing ingredients and producing fantastic food is where your head's at. The details of balance sheets, marketing plans and staff recruitment, training and management, and all the compliance regulations of health & safety, employment law, filing quarterly VAT returns and lots more leave you confused.

If you'd rather deal with a net of mussels than calculate net profit - this book's for you.

There are other trainers, lecturers and gurus out there who help people in the hospitality business – they have a vital role to play and this book is for them too – many trainers are excellent. Those who have done it, as well as talk about it, can be superb.

Top Tip

Becoming self-employed and taking on your own business, whether a café, restaurant or pub is a dream many bright-eyed, enthusiastic, entrepreneurial, would-be-restaurateurs hold dear to their heart. But, a word of caution before you rush out and exchange your life savings for the keys to your dream food business. Being self-employed may be your ultimate aspiration but it brings responsibilities and pitfalls you may not have considered in your previous 'PAYE employed person' status. Think these things through before you grab your P45 and the roses will still be around your door a year down the line.

For Doris

My Grandmother who was born in a pub in 1914, daughter of Innkeepers Sarah and William and who gave me the 'hospitality gene'.

First things first: CREATING THE MENU

Your checklist

- ✓ Write down all the fabulous dishes you will offer your customers
- ✓ Drool over recipe books and superhero chefs and incorporate some of their stuff as well as your favourite dishes
- ✓ Check out the competition and what they offer and vow to do it better
- ✓ Spend hours choosing the right shade of napkin and bud vase

Now, read this book and start again

1 Getting started

- Go back to basics – remind yourself why you're doing this
- Plan your income
- Size matters - so does location
- Who's cooking your books?
- What's so different about you – the nitty gritty?
- Five Profit Vampires that could throw you off course from Day One

2 Who's your customer?

- Suss out your target customers – without them you have no business
- What's a customer worth?
- When are you hungry and what can I feed you?
- Three Profit Vampires that will take your customers away with them

3 Planning a menu

- Create a menu that hits the spot 'food-wise' and 'price-wise'

- Accurately spec out your menu with costs and profit margins – boring but VITAL
- How to cost a dish
- Sub-recipe costing – even number gurus get this one wrong!
- How much to charge
- The menu as a hard selling tool
- Choosing the right words
- Pricing tricks
- Beware Seven tiny Profit Vampires and Nine Sunday Vampires

4 Attention to detail

- It's all about the food – or actually not
- Food makes you fat and allergic – you need to know this
- Your signature dish
- Variations on a theme – what are you going to be?
- Make it or buy it ready-made?
- Ten Profit Vampires that put your profits in the bin or in the staff

5 The other stuff – the stuff no-one tells you

- Don't be the best kept secret in town
- Try not to poison your customers
- Open your eyes to what your customers see
- The hidden detail
- 'I want to be alone' - George and Sonia syndrome
- Staff rule ok? 'Yes chef!'
- Hire slowly, fire quickly
- Service with a scowl – or a smile?
- 10 Profit Vampires your staff bring to the business

6 It's all about you

- Seven characteristics of successful operators
- Daily disciplines to build your business
- The ultimate secret to success

7 Templates and success blueprints

- Chef interview questions
- Customer profile questions
- Lifetime value of a customer
- Recipe Costing sheet
- Dish Costing sheet
- Menu writing check list
- 45 Marketing ways to promote your business
- Chef Incentive – how it works
- Chef Incentive – example tasks
- Chef Incentive – extra cash from extra GP
- Our Team Rocks – basic tasks checklist
- Our Team Rocks – customer WOW!
- 27 Golden Rules

Foreword

Back in the 1990's I was running a very foodie village pub with my then husband (and that in itself says much about the stress of managing a hospitality venue). We simply could not understand why, when we were very busy and had a sizeable turnover, we were not making the sort of profit we should have made. Actually, I'll be honest, in the early days we were pretty rubbish with the figures, made little or no profit and paid VAT with a credit card at one stage, we even came close to posting the keys back to the brewery.

But we didn't. Instead, we focused on the numbers and I embarked on an exercise that was to revolutionise the way I looked at food retail and the way we generated profit from our menu.

I knew that our lack of profit came from the way I managed (or rather didn't manage) the kitchen. So, dish-by-dish I weighed, counted and measured the recipes, the sub-recipes and the way we presented food on the plate. I scrutinised supplier prices, food waste and portion sizes. This was in the days when computers were the size of chests of drawers and the cloud was something that provided rain. It took me two solid weeks armed with scales and calculator. Equipped with all this information I made tiny tweaks and changes – substituting one ingredient for another, changing garnishes, standardising portions and reducing the size of my menu. The customers didn't notice a thing – the food to them was the same as it had always been – our bank manager on the other hand did notice the extra £10,000 we added to our bottom line that year. Who'd have thought that substituting one veg for another and presenting food on a different plate could make such an impact? That exercise taught me the importance of detail in a catering kitchen.

My background is in pubs and I make no apology for using examples from this industry throughout the book. Running a pub that serves food is one of the most complex businesses of the 21st Century. If your food operation isn't licensed or is much more niched – please don't dismiss this book as 'not for you'. In my opinion if you can successfully run a busy pub that does food – you are well equipped to run any sort of food operation (probably standing on your head!)

Since selling the Cornish pub/restaurant in 2007, I have established a hospitality training and software company called CaterCost.

CaterCost provides the ultimate cloud technology, menu management software and is the market leader for the independent sector. My motto is quite simply: '100% dedicated to making chefs happier and food businesses more profitable.'

1 Getting started

Back to Basics

'Remind me – why am I doing this?'

You need to be able to answer this...

You'll need to answer it today and at some time in the future when things go wrong, when you're on your knees with fatigue or you've really had about as much as you can take dealing with the general public!

Dig deep into your core.

If your answer includes phrases like 'I have a passion to create amazing food' or 'To create the best fish and chips in Macclesfield,' well, they're valid – but they aren't the correct answer to this question. If your answer is: 'My culinary talents will excite and satisfy a waiting market just desperate to sample my dishes' – well, that's fantastic for you, but this also is not the right answer.

If you answer that you are doing this for lifestyle reasons – to relocate away from the rat race or to create an ethical environment where everything is sourced and created with care and integrity, again this is wonderful news – a little rose-tinted maybe - but more on that later. However, it's still not the right answer.

If you have an unfulfilled dream that you are chasing, I applaud you, you will need to hold on to your dream and work hard to realise it, sadly it is still not the right answer.

The correct answer is 'to make money.'

The numbers, the cash and the profit!

The harsh truth is that whatever your personal ethical beliefs, lifestyle views or food passions, your number one focus needs to be on the cash. The journey into the world of hospitality needs to be taken with sound commercial savvy.

You need to accept that you are running a business – a commercial enterprise – and if you employ people they become dependent on you for their income and associated lifestyle. You therefore have as your number one priority a DUTY – yes a duty to make profit – for them and for you. A profitable business is a secure business and that takes away unimaginable pressures.

Profit first – fair enough if you believe that all animals should have a happy life and want your restaurant to serve only ethically-reared beef for example – that's absolutely fine, but you can't then expect to compete on price with the local fast food joint who buy in their meat for less than a quarter of the cost of yours.

- Successful food operators understand the importance of the numbers
- Successful food operators know down to the last penny what sales they have made today and what the cost of those sales has been today
- Successful food operators record this information and make it the focus of their decisions for every aspect of their business

Even if you swear blind that this is a 'lifestyle' choice for you and all you need is enough to get by, I promise you that at some point you will look with despair at the hours you are working, the responsibility and effort you have to put into every day, the way you pay your staff and your suppliers before yourself, and see how everyone seems to benefit from your endeavours – except you.

The lifestyle you want can only be sustained if there is enough profit left at the end of the day to reward yourself – even if it's just enough to give you a day off once in a while.

It's not my aim to turn every reader into a money-grabbing capitalist, exploiting workers and customers for selfish gain; it's just that if you truly understand your profit line life will be a much better experience for you.

You will no doubt be more successful and more profitable if you have integrity in your beliefs, food standards and dreams, but the number one reason for being in business is to make money and have a sustainable business. If you grasp this it will help you in your journey when you come to make tough decisions.

Golden Rule No.1

Focus on your numbers – you need to know your sales and costs every single day.

Plan your income

Begin with the end in mind

My former head chef Chris Adey, an incredibly talented and grounded guy, took the plunge six years ago to live the dream and set up his own restaurant. He fell in love with a fabulously located 'bistro' in Brixham and rushed to snap it up before the competition could move in. With hindsight he freely admits to what I call 'roses round the door' syndrome. His emotional attachment to the place took precedence over the numbers – WRONG! With his talents he was very quickly bursting at the seams, but he only had 24 covers. Expansion to the next-door vacant outlet didn't stack up as it would double his key overheads for just another 20 or so seats. Now, frustratingly stuck in a business where he knows that however hard he works (and he is one of the hardest workers I know) he will never make the money he deserves to make while he is limited by space.

Know your numbers backwards

One of the biggest mistakes new food operators make is one of scale. They end up buying places that are simply too small to generate the level of reward they seek.

Before you sign on the dotted line ask yourself this question:

'What do I want in terms of money/revenue from my business in exchange for the hours I'm going to work?'

Knowing what you want to be left with after all the bills are paid is the first step to understanding the size of restaurant, cafe or pub you need to run. Put simply, this number will determine the turnover you must have, to generate the margins you will need, to meet the rent/mortgage, wage costs and overheads and still leave a surplus for your remuneration.

Size matters

(So does location)

Let's say that you think small and manageable. If you are successful it will be costly as you struggle on a limited budget with the restrictions of a small premises to expand the business to meet demand and create more wealth for yourself.

If you think small and do OK that's all you'll ever achieve.

Ignore the 'roses round the door' emotional attachment you have to your chosen restaurant, pub or café and face some hard business facts: size matters. You will limit your potential income if you choose too small.

You may try to convince yourself 'it will be manageable,' 'I won't need staff,' 'I can do it all myself' but try telling that to your future self when you haven't had a day off in the last two and a half years.

Size basics

The number of covers you can serve will put a ceiling on your turnover.

Example:

Say your operation has five tables that seat four, a table of three and one of two. That's a total of 25 seats or 'covers' as they are known in the trade. Say, you only open in the evening.

Your maximum weekly turnover will be 25 x 7 x average spend per head.

If average spend per head including drinks is £15 – you will have maximum weekly takings of £2,625.

Ask yourself honestly - is this enough? Don't forget you will need to allow for VAT from this figure (unless you are a cold takeaway). At the time of writing the VAT rate was 20% and in this case reduces those weekly takings by £438.

VAT is payable on all food served in restaurants and other food businesses exceeding a turnover of £79,000 per year. It is vital to understand this when putting a menu together to ensure the 20% you will have to pay to the Government (as an unpaid tax collector) does not compromise your desired profit margin. See Chapter 3 to work out VAT using a formula.

You can of course, if you want no quality of life, increase your sales by extending the hours you open to include breakfast, lunch, afternoon tea and late night takeaway. You can also look at a more casual eating-out offer where you can 'turn' the tables and get more than one set of diners per table per occasion:

25 covers x lunch @ £8 per head	£200
12 turned table covers at lunch @ £8 per head	£96
25 covers x dinner @ £15 per head	£375
12 turned table covers at dinner @ £15 per head	£180
25 breakfasts @ £5 a head	£125
25 afternoon teas @ £5 a head	£125
20 takeaway meals @ £4 per head	£80

If you were able to achieve capacity in this way (personal stamina permitting), your daily takings would be £1,181 which, less VAT = £985 per day, or £6,895 per week, totalling £360,000 per year (assuming this business was open and full to capacity every single day, 365 days a year!)

If you were to do it all yourself and crack this number of covers you would have an exhausting lifestyle, with long hours and little respite to restock the kitchen and prepare the food; if you're not 'hands-on' and employ people to do it for you, you will generate a wage bill that will soon eat into your profits.

What's in it for you?

First of all you have to pay for the food and drink that you buy in to prepare and serve to your customers. This may cost you 35% of your turnover - it may be a bit more or a bit less, but 35% food and drink costs is a realistic figure.

You may then have to cover staff and overheads. What you are hoping is that these expenses amount to no more than 55% of your turnover - less for preference! That way you are left with 10% net profit. This is your hard earned cash reward, but don't forget you will need to make provision to pay your personal tax from this figure. This means that on a net turnover of £360,000 like this you could end up taking home between £17,000 and £27,000 a year.

This is fine if your eyes are wide open, but not so good if you have dreams of a yacht in the Caribbean.

Given that the likely turnover in this particular example is more realistically going to be half this figure - you can do the sums to work out your potential income.

Numbers don't lie

The truth is – numbers don't lie – if it doesn't work on paper it won't work in reality.

You can only really come up with sensible predictions and budgets if you know what you're aiming for in terms of your costs and overheads:

- Food Costs
- Staff Costs
- Utilities
- Rent and Rates
- Other Overheads

Top Tip

Setting annual targets for sales can seem a bit daunting as the numbers can seem too big to deal with. Break sales targets down to weekly sales targets and then break these down into daily sales targets.

Doing this makes things much more manageable – and a lot less scary! 'Can I increase profit by £2,500 a year?' becomes 'Can I sell another four coffees a day?'

Golden Rule No.2

Decide what you want to earn - then use this to decide what size business (or businesses) you will need to operate to generate your desired income. It needs to be big enough to earn you a decent living/make you a fortune*

*delete as appropriate

Location

Everyone will tell you 'Location, Location, Location'

And while there are exceptions that we can all think of that buck this rule, for example, the three Michelin-starred Fat Duck which is basically in a terraced house on Bray high street while the equally three-starred Waterside Inn is a mile or so away perched in a beautiful spot beside the Thames.

There are three and a half things you need to consider once you have decided on the scale of your operation

1.   **Investigate the demographics of the area** - basically who lives there, what social type are they, how many kids, you get the picture. Try:
www.checkmyarea.com.
www.businessballs.com/demographicsclassifications.htm
www.acorn.caci.co.uk
www.experian.co.uk

Doing this can be as simple or as complex as you want to make it, what you're basically trying to figure out is how much disposable income your potential customers have and how your proposed offer fits in with this.

I know of one successful operator with several outlets who quite simply looks at a prospective town and if there's a Waitrose then he knows that town will be suitable for his food offer. Others invest in detailed demographic reports available online from various companies. The point is that there has to be enough of your target market in the area and you need to check it out. 'Keeping your fingers crossed' or going on 'gut feel' may prove a poor option. Obviously, local knowledge is a distinct advantage.

You can actually do a lot of this yourself. For example, working out the proportion of closed/charity/high street chains/thriving independents? What are people wearing? Are they carrying lots of shopping bags – and are they from John Lewis, H&M or Poundland?

2.   **Check out the competition** - there is an argument for locating near to your biggest competitor and other similar businesses.
Think of the industrial estates and retail parks that have created 'go-to' areas where customers can pop from one furniture store to another. You need to be confident enough in your offer to outsell your competitors but being close to the competition can have the added advantage of 'piggy-backing' on to the marketing they are doing to drive customers to their doors.

3.   **Travel** - consider how people are going to get to you and make it easy for them. Ease of accessibility is crucial; this covers parking, public transport and even how easy it is for suppliers to deliver.

3½.   **Think expansion** – if it's successful is there scope for your trade to grow?

Who's cooking your books?

Before they hand you the keys get a good accountant

After a rather disastrous management account company left us with an unnecessary tax bill I sought a new accountant and on the recommendation of another businessman I found Michael. Rather than simply take my business and let me engage him to manage our financial affairs, he actually interviewed me – just like a job interview - before deciding whether he wanted me as a client.

This may seem a strange – but it actually was genius - a sign that he took the client relationship seriously. The one thing that was truly important was that he wouldn't work with people he didn't like, who were only 'playing' businesses and were not serious about what they did. He turned out to be absolutely invaluable – like an additional member of the team, always involved with planning a financial strategy and never just rocking up when it was tax return signing time! He set the bar high for other accountants that have followed.

With the numbers playing such a core role in your business you will be ill-advised to set off on your catering journey without an accountant to help you manage the financials.

There are plenty of practical guides out there to help you tick all the compliance boxes, like informing the Inland Revenue that you are now self-employed and registering for VAT with HM Customs & Excise. This book includes the stuff they don't tell you.

One of these things is that you absolutely need to get yourself a good accountant. Other guides merely tell you to 'get an accountant' – it's getting a GOOD one that's the hard bit. One of life's mysteries is that as a nation the UK has more accountants per capita than anywhere else in the world, and yet I seldom speak to anyone who truly rates their own accountant.

As a minimum they must be able to give you rapid feedback so you can track your profits monthly at the very least. They should also help you plan your cash flow and tax liability as part of the deal. A good accountant will be proactive with practical and money-saving advice as the business grows and before the tax bill arrives.

An accountant that only contacts you once a year will not help you.

Seven things to ask your accountant

1.   How does my business compare to my competitors?

2.   Is my gross profit* reasonable for my type of business?

3.   How much net profit** is my business making and is it worth the effort I'm putting in?

4.   What's my most profitable income stream?

5.   What can I do to improve my cash flow?

6.   How much money do I have invested in my business that could be better invested somewhere else?

7.   Is my business in a good financial position? Could I survive a downturn?

A good accountant will have the answers to these and demonstrate a true understanding of your business. My current accountant, Roger, is so good he provided me with these questions!

*Gross Profit (GP) = total sales less the cost of sales (the buying price of food and drink that you sell)

**Net Profit (NP) = GP less the cost of everything else (staff costs, utilities, operating costs). This is your 'Bottom Line.'

What's so different about you?

The nitty gritty – you and the outgoing operator?

Pubs in particular suffer a lot from changes in operator - a change of landlord and landlady can spell disaster. When I was in my late 20s I went to work at a village pub restaurant – the outgoing landlady had recently sold this very successful bistro-style country pub, with a fabulous fresh food offer, to a couple who had run town pubs and knew little of the niceties of village life. Soon signs went up saying 'no muddy boots' and 'we charge 50p for taking cheques' (yes it was a long time ago) and fresh food was replaced with convenience ready meals. The casual cosy atmosphere was stifled by 'rules' and shirts and ties The first night they opened they were rammed, I worked as hard as I'd done at a six deep student union bar, but I never saw the bar that busy again under their ownership. Trade dropped away and dwindled to nothing. They left after just one year.

When a food business changes hands there are usually two scenarios:

Taking over a success

Picture a thriving, busy outlet with established menus and food trade, trained staff and well-presented premises. Most new operators going in usually think they are buying a goldmine, 'a licence to print money' which will involve very little personal effort on their part. Sadly in these cases people often haven't grasped how many small and unnoticed things are done every day to sustain the high level of success. If they're not careful, the place simply doesn't feel the same, run the same or trade the same.

If you are taking over a successful operation you must pay very close attention to the detail. It's never one big thing but lots of tiny particulars, for example, ambient lighting, music selection, temperature, staff - the list is endless. (See context of the sale in Chapter 5).

Time and time again I have seen the fortunes of businesses spiral downwards with the owners completely in the dark as to why. The information contained in these pages will make sure that's not you.

Taking over a dive

Picture a run-down outlet where the outgoing operators have struggled to make a living, haven't been able to invest in the fabric of the premises, equipment, staff or marketing and are desperate to hand over the keys of their broken dream. Three things can happen:

1. **The new operators have a 'vision** - they're going to change the place – do it up, do it differently. They are backed with sufficient capital to invest in renovation and an unwavering belief that they will succeed in transforming the place. They focus on the important stuff, they take responsibility for their actions and they identify the right target market. They create an offer that is right for their target market, market themselves properly and they end up with a swanky house and Audi convertible.

2. **The new operator carries on like the outgoing owner** - thinking that continuing to do the same thing will somehow, for them, magically produce a different set of results. They are under-funded and do everything from a cost perspective – not from a 'customer experience' perspective. They change little and put their faith in the hope that people will come, without any real understanding of who those people are and what they really want when they get there.

3. **The new operators finds themselves at a loss** – wondering what to do with the place, wishing they had asked more questions and delved a bit deeper as to the reasons why trade hasn't worked here. If only they had asked why the place has seen several owners and several re-inventions of style, cuisine and décor and yet still never made a success of things. If they had they wouldn't have wasted so much time trying out new ideas only to fail expensively. Generally speaking if it was once good it can probably be good again in new hands, but finding what to change without research, clear vision and a written business plan with goals set against specific dates is more trial and error than is financially healthy.

Golden Rule No.3

You plan to be successful don't you? So ask yourself: 'Is it scalable? If your food is popular with customers and creates a big demand, will you outgrow your premises too soon? Relocation or expansion costs will quickly eat into your early profits.

BEWARE the Profit Vampires that will throw you off course from Day One

No.1 Not thinking big

A commercial kitchen should always be too big for your needs so there is room for you to grow into it as trade develops and your business grows. If it is small you will forever be adding bits to storage and prep areas to keep up with the growing number of covers. This will be expensive and invasive

No.2 Focusing on the pretty things

and not on the core numbers. Exciting as it may be (and essential) to get carried away with the 'look and feel' of your business the core numbers of the business need to take priority

No.3 Falling in love

Taking on a restaurant or pub based on an emotional attachment made to the business rather than a levelheaded business decision, the 'roses-round-the-door' syndrome will lead you to be blind to some of the failings of the premises and location.

No.4 Not doing your homework

Hand-in-hand with 'roses-round-the-door syndrome' is 'not doing your homework' before you sign on the dotted line. With the easy availability of all sorts of information and guidance on the Internet, it is only a lazy or stupid operator who doesn't thoroughly research their premises.

No.5 Choosing the wrong accountant

Engaging an accountant that you don't really like, who only wants to see you once a year and who doesn't really understand the nuances of the hospitality industry. You will only succeed if you have a positive and proactive relationship with your accountant

2 Who's your customer?

Suss out your customer

Without customers you have no business...

One business that we bought, and transformed to become highly profitable, was located a few miles up from the popular Cornish town of Padstow, where Rick Stein had been quietly creating a destination food village and where nearby Rock and Fistral Beach were seeing the emergence of the new style gastro pubs. At the time the Bay View Inn – beautifully located overlooking a surfing beach and yet stuck in a time-warp that catered to the bucket and spade end of the market – was cost-focused. This meant Cash & Carry ingredients and unimaginative menu standards appealing to the cheaper end of the market on holiday at the local camp sites, budget holiday parks and in the winter the local inhabitants of Bude and surrounding villages.

Bearing in mind that Cornwall was one of the poorest counties in Britain at the time it seemed obvious to keep catering for this customer base. However, by researching the customer more deeply we stumbled upon a customer profile that was far more lucrative for us and enabled us to create an offer that appealed specifically to them. What we found was a whole bunch of well-heeled professional families that were visiting Cornwall four, five, six times a year for long weekends and mid-week breaks. These people travelled from London, the Shires and Home Counties and unlike the cash-strapped budget families, they were interested in quality food.

This was at a time of important changes in British hospitality and catering, with the upmarket sandwich chain Pret a Manger beginning to flourish, the start of farmers markets selling locally grown and organic foods and M&S greatly expanding its excellent food offering. Our newly-marketed customer base were M&S and Waitrose shoppers and were fed-up finding the same low-grade food in many pubs and restaurants when they visited Cornwall.

By identifying what was important to this group we were among the first local businesses to create a food offer based around locally sourced quality products. The effect? We quadrupled food sales in two years.

We couldn't have done that if we'd stayed focusing on the food aspirations of the target market in our immediate location and kept our offer the same. The interesting thing was that as word spread we became an aspirational 'treat' venue for the low-budget holiday makers and a destination for the Londoners who were selling up in London and relocating for a 'lifestyle' choice in the West Country.

Who's the right target market for you?

It's worth spending a considerable amount of time contemplating who will be your target market.

Who will be your customer is linked to location. Think - a posh French-cuisine styled restaurant in an inner city housing estate? Or a greasy spoon in a wealthy Home Counties village? These are never going to be winning businesses. Knowing your customers inside out is a business foundation stone that must be laid at the very start and re-visited every month as trends change. Whether you're at the planning stage, just got started or have a well-established customer base, it is still worth giving a lot of thought to who your customers really are.

Nothing can be more fundamental to the success or failure of a restaurant, pub kitchen or food-serving establishment than having a deep insight into the lives of your target customer.

Until you understand where they shop, go on holiday, what newspapers they read, what social media platforms they use, what sports and teams they take part in and support, what they love, what they hate, what they fear and what they strive for, can you identify the sort of food offer and associated environment that is going to appeal specifically to them.

'Build it and they will come!' I'd rather say: 'Know them inside out and they won't be able to resist coming!'

Once you understand the customer base you want to attract, you can start to understand their buying habits.

Food Occasions

Different food occasions and opportunities for your target groups need to be studied. Once you know your target groups of customer (the more of these you can identify, the stronger your business will be) you can benchmark your building, your facilities, your staff and your food and drink with revealing questions: 'Would Tony and Beth like the car parked here in the muddy field, would they be able to navigate their way up these steps and find the entrance even though there is no clear signage?'

You need to ask yourself: 'Is every aspect of my offer making it easy for Tony and Beth to do business with me?' If where they can park is important to them (if they've got a swanky car it will be – if they catch the bus it won't – but a nearby bus stop will be) you will be able to fix it.

In Chapter 7 there is a template to create a customer profile. Bring them to life, give them a name and be as specific as you can.

You can create as many customer profile templates as you like, particularly if you wish to attract different types of customers at different times of the day, the week and the year.

How to create a customer profile:

1. Give them a name

2. Are they male or female?

3. How old are they?

4. What do they do during the day?

5. What do they do in the evenings?

6. What do they do at the weekends?

7. What paper do they read?

8. What sport do they play?

9. What sport do they follow?

10. Where do they shop for food and drink?

11. What do they like to drink?

12. What hobbies do they have?

13. Do they use the internet? (If not, why waste time on email marketing?)

14. Do they use social media? (ditto above)

15. Are they health conscious?

16. Where do they go on holiday?

17. What car do they drive?

The list is as long as you want to make it as the more detail you have about the lives of your customers, the more you can craft your offer to appeal to them.

Top Tip.

It is no coincidence that Tesco – one of the super successful supermarkets of the early 2000's - rose to the top effortlessly after the introduction of its Clubcard. Tesco understood earlier than most that knowing the purchasing habits of their customers not only enabled them to create irresistible offers for them but also to create a demographic picture nationwide to help develop the stores.
In fact, the introduction of the Tesco Clubcard was the single most significant factor in the success of the company, says Sir Terry Leahy, the supermarket's chief executive from 1997 to 2011.
Through Clubcard, Tesco collected raw data on what people were buying and turned it into profitable information. It was also able to offer personalised discounts and rewards. Rolled out nationally in 1995, the card was an instant success. One year later Tesco became the UK's top supermarket and at one stage one pound in every seven spent in British shops went into a Tesco till!
The scheme fundamentally changed the way all supermarkets did business and typifies Tesco's success say business analysts. Leahy is quoted as saying: 'We discovered more about our customers in a week than in the previous 50 years.'

Golden Rule No.4

Without customers you have no business. Knowing your target customers inside out will give you a head start over your competition. In-depth customer analysis isn't rocket science – but not bothering to really match your offer to your target audience is bonkers.

What's a customer worth?

Lifetime value of a customer – what will you spend on marketing to get a new one?

This is a tale about stealing success from the jaws of defeat. On an ordinary Saturday evening I was in the kitchen when the chef was asked to re-cook a steak for a customer who'd complained. We handled the complaint graciously and generously and the re-cooked steak was given free and a round of drinks bought for the group of diners. Little did we know that was probably the best PR/marketing spend we had ever made. Now, giving drinks away is not generally a good idea, but they seemed non-professional complainers (you get to know the sort who do it and expect not to pay) and we had genuinely made a mistake. It cost us around £30 to make lifetime customers of this couple who from that moment on loved us. All we'd done was care enough to want them to have a great time while they were with us and when we made a mistake we tried to put it right as best we could. What they did was return every single Saturday without fail, always with another couple – sometimes a group of friends – spending upwards of £100 a visit. They came with new and old friends – all of whom in turn became frequent visitors and bought other people to spend money with us. One of these visitors hired the whole restaurant for all his friends on his 50th – they were all local and became customers until the day we sold.

How much?

This is a very valuable exercise to do as understanding the worth of every customer to your business allows you to make some pretty sophisticated decisions about the money (marketing budget) you are prepared to spend to get more customers like them.

This example highlights how you can set yourself apart from your competitors who always think how they can spend the least on marketing to attract custom – and seldom get beyond an ad in the paper or a flyer through the door.

Firstly, consider a customer (this may be a real live customer or a target customer that you would like to have). In this instance let's call them Andy and Kae – they're in their late fifties and eat out regularly.

They visit your restaurant twice a month on a Saturday night and spend £50 on average each time. They've been doing this for the last four years and will probably carry on as customers unless they move out of the area, die or defect to another restaurant. For the sake of this example let's say they stay for another 15 years. They also have a couple of big family 'dos' with you twice a year and spend £350 each time.

What does this mean? Well Andy and Kae are worth approximately £38,000 to your business over their buying lifetime 26 (visits per year) x £50 (average spend) + £700 (2 special occasions) x 19 (number of years they're your customer).

However it doesn't stop there

This is the bit that most people don't appreciate: happy customers tell their friends and family about nice places to eat and drink. They may bring them as guests one evening and then these guests come on their own as they too become your customers.

Andy and Kae sometimes bring another couple with them, Sylvia and Rich. As well as dining with you every other Saturday with Andy and Kae, Sylvia and Rich come in every Sunday with their family and spend £100. Sylvia's daughter Charlotte also visits you (apart from Sundays) with her girlfriends once a month and spends £40 and Charlotte's hubby comes in a couple of times a week for a business lunch at £10 a time

This means the collective value of Andy and Kae's friends and associates is £7,980 per year;

26 (visits per year) x £50 (average spend) with Andy and Kae = £1,300
52 (visits on Sunday) x £100 (average spend) with their family = £5,200
12 (Charlotte and her girlfriends visits) x £40 = £480
100 (Charlottes' hubby's business lunches) x £10 = £1,000

If this activity carries on for, say, six years (£47,880) THE

TRUE VALUE of Andy and Kae as customers is £85,880 over their buying lifetime.

NOW, armed with this information, can't you afford to be just a bit more creative than an ad in the paper and a poster in the window to try and attract more customers of the same profile as Andy and Kae?

Surely if someone has a lifetime value to you of £85k you could really WOW them with your marketing offer. Would you pay out a couple of hundred quid to get another Andy and Kae? Yes of course you would. This exercise empowers you, for example, you could offer a completely free birthday meal for six (cost to you under £100) to the right target customer. If they convert to becoming regular diners you potentially get £85k over their buying lifetime.

Your competition will not understand this concept of investment in marketing. Once you grasp it, your marketing to attract new custom will take on a whole new dimension. See '45 Marketing Tips to Promote Your Business' in Chapter 7 for more ideas.

When are you hungry?

...and what can I feed you?

I once worked with a publican who was not doing any food at all. We were looking at trading patterns and ways to increase turnover. Discussing a typical day he explained how his bar was usually pretty empty by 10pm most nights as customers disappeared after having their takeaway pizza delivery dropped at the pub before they went home. I asked him how often this happened and how many customers did this. It turned out to be every day. Suddenly the penny dropped. He realised that he was giving away literally thousands of pounds worth of easy food trade at high gross profit to the local pizza place. This was an opportunity to increase his own revenue that he had completely overlooked.

Find the food opportunity

The more opportunities there are for customers to eat with you the better. Even if you are a special occasion dining outlet – take a closer look to see if you're making the most of all-day grazing that has become the norm in the UK.

Food opportunities aren't necessarily obvious at first glance. Someone may be a self-confessed 'fresh foodie' but on a Saturday night is quite happy to tuck into a delicious fat-oozing doner kebab on the way home from the match. The woman who is on an eternal diet and really picky and health conscious may want the opportunity for a naughty slice of cake on the way back from the gym. The Saturday night 'fine diner' may love nothing better than a nice pizza takeaway mid-week. So, don't just ask yourself 'what do they like?' but also 'what's their guilty pleasure?'

Food for every occasion

Only once you get to grips with this can you develop an offer that's going to appeal. We are creatures of habit – many of us eating similar things for lunch every single day – and having a repertoire of only five dishes that we alternate for our main meals.

The trick is to balance the familiar and the popular dishes with something your customer base can't or won't cook at home but will still really like. For example, meals with sauces and food that need proper cooking skills and fiddly preparation.

Your food offer will probably need to be different things to different groups at different times of the day, week and year. Generally the more food occasion there are in your business the more reasons there are for your loyal customers to visit you more frequently. For example, a pub may have all the following food occasions:

- Breakfast – networking groups and manual workers
- Morning - cakes and coffee for mums and toddlers after dropping off the kids at school
- Lunch deals Mon to Thurs - OAPs
- Lunch - fast food for office workers. University of Westminster research says the average time taken to eat lunch nowadays is 15 minutes
- Afternoon tea – grannies, shoppers and friends
- Early doors (5-7pm) - tapas snacks to soak up a pint on the way home
- Dinner menu
- Special nights Mon-Thurs – Curry, Steak, 'Two for £10'
- Saturday football - deluxe burger and chips
- Sunday morning brunch
- Sunday Lunch - families
- Sunday - All You Can Eat buffet night
- All day – casual dining and grazing

The trend in the UK is definitely moving away from 'three square meals a day' to a culture of 'all-day grazing.' Reasons cited include work and family pressures and, in 1986, the launch of the first microwave meals was said to have been the beginning of the end for the evening family meal round the table.

Profit Vampires that will lure your customers away

No.6 Not knowing your customer

Only when you truly know your target customer can you provide those tiny details to make them feel they genuinely belong at your establishment. That 'special dish' on the menu that reminds them of holiday; that magazine to read while they wait for their friends; that brand of soap in the loos that they love; the background music that's playing….. the list is endless

No.7 Being sniffy about food

Ignoring opportunities to provide customers food because it's outside your core offer – let's face it you can buy a sandwich in a chemist, a garden centre and a petrol station – so why can't you provide take-home Chinese food or pizza from an English Bistro?

No.8 Not appreciating lifetime value

Not appreciating the lifetime value of a loyal customer and building/creating customer 'loyalty' into your core business values and way of working.

3 Planning the menu

Create a menu

A menu that hits the spot food-wise and price-wise

I've always been intrigued as to why (with a handful of exceptions) vegetarian restaurants don't work. I guess it's because non-vegetarians go out to eat with vegetarians and get fed-up (or not fed at all) because there are no meat dishes. We are still a nation of meat eaters. The statistics vary wildly on the actual number of veggies from 0.3% of the population to 7%, but the truth is that if you're setting-up or running a food operation you will be catering for the UK's meat eaters. So when creating your menu by all means have some veggie options, having quite a few imaginative ones is a good move, but you will need to consider two things:

'Most meals are simply a bit of protein wrapped in a bit of carb, topped with something yummy, there may or may not be a bit of vegetation on the side.'

And, according to Ray Kroc – founder of McDonalds: 'All customers care about is having tasty, cheap food served to them cleanly, consistently and quickly.'

If you replace the word 'cheap' with 'good value' these two sentences pretty much sum up the template for the food offer of a 21st Century restaurant.

Despite the seemingly vast array of variations on food, when you strip away the trappings of the dining-out world you are left with pretty much the same thing. It's actually not that complicated.

Top Tip

Successful menus usually involve dishes that are difficult to re-create at home.

How to plan the dishes on your menu

Whatever style of operation:

Start with the protein element of the dish – this is usually the most expensive part. If you are creating a fixed menu you will need to ensure that the protein elements involved are not subject to price fluctuations during the life of the menu or this will affect your profitability. If necessary, cut a deal with your supplier to fix a price for the given period.

Once you have your protein sorted, consider the carbohydrate element. This will give the satisfying tummy-full factor for your customers, as it will add bulk to the meal. The carb element can also be used to add perceived value on the plate.

Next the fun bit: the flavour will come in the slop – the sauce, the yummy stuff with spices, herbs and basics like garlic, onion or even mustard in a sandwich.

Lastly, consider the vegetation – fresh veg and salad takes a lot of prep, has a high wastage factor (peelings, prep time and short shelf life). On the plus side they look pretty on the plate – add flavour and texture and a 'healthy' balance to the meal. On the down side – if the customers don't eat them and they end up discarded you might just as well be throwing your money in the bins.

And while we may want to try and break from this formula and provide 'niche' alternatives we must bear in mind consumer demands.

Golden Rule No.5

Say to yourself: 'I am not my customer. Whatever my own personal feelings about food, I will provide the food my customers want to eat.'

Spec out your menu with costs and profit margins

– boring but VITAL

Now you can spend hours deliberating on the mouth-watering dishes you will tempt your customers with, but before you do it's worth looking closely at two other things:

What price are your customers willing to pay?

This will determine the quality of ingredients you can use and therefore the suppliers you will need – if you want to make a profit that is.

What is the skill set of your cook, chef and kitchen team?

This will determine the level of complexity of your dishes.

Price and gross profit

When we first took the Cornish pub/restaurant with letting rooms, my target GP was only 40% for six months – this was deliberate but by setting it low I was still able to buy top quality ingredients and 'over-deliver' on customers' food expectations. Once they were hooked on the food and coming back time and time again I stealthily increased the prices through introducing new menus and drilling down on my buying costs.

Sometimes taking a hit on GP% is a smart move and an effective way to market the business.

Getting your pricing WRONG is really easy to do

For those of you who are really confident you have the Gross Profit thing all sorted please feel free to skip this bit, but you'd be amazed how many intelligent business folk there are out there who are just a little sketchy on these numbers.

Before you start setting out your dishes and their retail price points you need to look closely at the basic rule of retail.

You buy something at a cost price and resell it in your environment (shop, café, restaurant, pub) for more than you paid for it. The difference between the cost price and the selling price is known as GROSS PROFIT.

Example:

I buy a loaf of bread from a wholesaler for 50p
I sell the loaf in my shop for £1.25
The GP I make is 75p (selling price £1.25 – 50p = 75p)
The GP expressed as a percentage is 60% (75p/125p x 100)
The mark-up is 150% (The retail price is one and a half times the cost of the loaf)

In the food industry we have the additional complication of VAT, which is generally payable on all menu items. The calculation details are later in this chapter.

Things get complicated when you venture into the realms of takeaway food. At the time of writing, as a general rule, if food is heated and being kept warm in the premises, or is intended to be served hot, such as a spit roasted chicken, then VAT is payable. If it is being left to cool at room temperature or is cold, then no VAT is payable. This is a very litigious area and in May 2012 the government did a U-turn on the so-called 'Pasty Tax' so please visit www.customs.hmrc.gov.uk for up-to-date information.

GROSS PROFIT:

This can be summed up as: sale price less direct cost of sale

NET PROFIT:

This is what you are left with after you have paid all your overheads and running costs (rent, rates, staff etc.) out of your gross profit.

Setting and achieving accurate GROSS PROFIT margins IS fundamental to achieving your desired NET PROFIT.

When you create your menu it is essential you have some idea of what GP margin you want to make. This doesn't have to be a fixed number for every dish – but an overall number based on a sales mix. If you don't start with this number you might as well forget about being a successful business owner as really this is what it's all about.

Top Tip

It's widely recognised that 60–70% GP for food outlets is the norm for the industry but there are so many variables according to your style of operation, location and food type that is silly to try and generalise too much.

There are places that use food as a driver to get people through the door with special offers. They are prepared to lower their food GP in order to drive sales on other products such as drink or accommodation. The point is that your understanding and policy on GPs are a deliberate and conscious decision and part of your business plan and structure – not something you have left to chance while 'hoping for the best.'

Golden Rule No.6

Spend time on the boring stuff – costing your menu and setting the right margins for all the food you sell is VITAL and the lengths you go to will make or break your business.

How to cost a dish

The simplest way to do this is to calculate the cost per gram or ml of a specific ingredient and multiply this figure by the quantity used in the recipe or dish.

- You need to know the weight or volume of the ingredient as it is purchased (this will be written on the packet or on the invoice for the product)
- You need to know the cost of that ingredient (for that specified weight or volume) this will be found on the invoice or price list
- You will probably need a calculator!

Example

1 kg of sugar costs £0.99

To work out cost per gram

£0.99 divided by 1000 (number of grams in a kilo) = 0.00099p per g

Next you need to work out the cost of the amount of that ingredient you are using in your dish specification or recipe

Say your recipe uses 350g of sugar

To work this out you take the price for 1g of sugar (0.00099p) and multiply this figure by 350 (the number of grams in your recipe)
The calculation is as follows:
0.00099 x 350 = 0.3465 - rounded up = £0.35 (or 35p)

Formula

1. Cost of ingredient (purchase quantity) £/p

2. Divided by weight or volume of purchase ingredient in grams or millilitres

3. Multiplied by weight or volume used in dish in grams or millilitres

4. Equals cost of quantity used in the recipe or dish of that specific ingredient

Batch Size

For a recipe you will need to determine the total batch size (finished quantity of the bulk recipe) you are making.

E.g. this recipe makes 30 kg – 40 portions of 750g

For many recipes don't forget to factor in shrinkage for meat or evaporation for sauces and stews.

For example, a roast joint of beef may have a raw weight of 5 kilos and cost £35 or £7 per kilo or 0.007p per g

Once cooked the servable weight of this joint is 4 kilos after 20% is wasted in the cooking process. This means that 4 kilos has cost you £35 or £8.75 per kilo or 0.00875p per gram

This is important.

If you cost the dish using the cost of the raw weight your figures will be inaccurate and make it impossible to achieve an actual GP in practice that matches the theoretical GP of your costings.

Using the roast meat example above, if you serve 200g portions of roast beef you will get 20 portions from this joint at a cost of £1.75 per portion - 200 x 0.00875 or £35 divided by 20

If you had not allowed for wastage you would be working to the wrong cost based only on raw meat of £1.40

Once you have calculated all the ingredient costs you need to add them up to make a total recipe or dish cost.

To calculate how much you need to sell this item for on the menu follow the formula later in this chapter.

Sub-recipe costing

Even the number gurus get this one wrong

I presented to a group of senior management executives at a prestigious food and beverage company. These guys were at the top of their game with years of combined industry experience between them. I asked them to cost a made-from-scratch burger. I presented the information in the way an operator would generally receive it - from invoices and price lists.

They laughed at me – these men and women knew one end of a spreadsheet from another.

The Food Costing Challenge I gave them:

It's quite simple – using the recipe and purchasing info below, how much does each 6oz beef burger patty cost?

All I told them was the recipe makes 40 x 6oz portions.

Guess what – after 20 minutes only one person out of 12 came close to an answer!

Here's the Recipe for 'Home-Made Beef Burger Patty'

- 12lb minced beef - the butcher's invoice gives the price as £5.49 per kilo
- 8 onions - 2.5 kilos of onions costs £2.50, one onion weighs 215g
- 4 eggs - 60 eggs cost £6.99
- 4 cups home-made breadcrumbs - 3 loaves of bread make 1lb of breadcrumbs
- 5 tsp beef bouillon - 2 kg costs £25.99
- 2 cups chopped parsley - 1 bunch (125g) parsley with stalks £1.26 – 45% waste
- 1 tbsp cracked black pepper - 600g costs £7.69
- 2 tsp salt - 6 kg costs £4.63
- 5 cloves garlic - 12 bulbs costs £4.25, (1 bulb = 7 cloves, 1 clove = 5 g)

The notion that we are all metric with standardised info and computerised is nonsense and only adds complexity. The reality is that suppliers' invoices (to which most operators refer if they are trying to cost an item) are a mish-mash of hand written and computerised, metric and imperial.

- We buy meat in kilos and still put an 8oz steak on the menu
- We buy herbs as a bunch but only use a pinch
- We buy 25kg of onions but use a single onion in a recipe

After the executives attempted to cost the burger patty, I pointed out that the fun doesn't stop there. To get the dish onto the plate and arrive at an accurate cost with nutritional value, they would need to cost other 'sub-recipes' such as 'home-made salad dressing', 'home-made chutney' and 'home-made mayonnaise' as these are other recipes within the 'Burger and Chips' and must be calculated before the dish can be given an on-the-plate cost.

They would also need to know the cost of the burger bun (bought in 8's) the cost of a slice of onion, the cost of a garnish (lettuce, half a tomato, 3 slices of cucumber etc) and the size and cost of a portion of chips (oil, salt etc).

Once this is done the calculation is:

Cost price divided by (100 – desired gross profit) x 100 x 1.2 = retail price

I then asked these big company hot-shots to try getting the nutritional info for this exact burger. No-one knew where to start.

With this in mind, and the complexity of the calculations for one simple dish on the menu, it's not surprising many operators make the big mistake of guessing the food costs.

Golden Rule No.7
Guessing food costs and profit margins is not an option.
'Food costing is an exact science.'

Technology has moved on and now with a cloud-hosted system CaterCost makes crunching these numbers a breeze. Check out www.catercost.com and take the 48-hour free trial to see just how easy it is to create a fully-costed and nutritionally analysed dish specs and menus.

How much to charge?

Copying the competition isn't a good strategy

Some people decide on the food they want to put on the menu, decide on the quality they want that food to be (local produce, free-range, ready meals) and then set the menu prices to achieve the GP they want, with scant regard for the disposable spend of their target clientele.

Others list all the dishes they want on their menu, look around at the competition to see what they sell their similar/comparable dishes for, and either copy, or go a little bit cheaper.

There are two flaws with this approach:

Focusing too much on the food without considering your target customer in the area will be disastrous. You may think Gloucester Old Spot dry-cured ham sandwich on organic grain bread, Duchy of Cornwall meadow-farmed butter, selected rocket leaves with imported mustard commands the hefty £10.99 price tag you need to make 65% GP. The harsh fact is that if your target customer only has £4 to spend on lunch, they will probably pick up a ham sarnie from the local garage or Boots for a couple of quid rather than rush to you.

Copying the competition is risky. Your customers may be happy to pay a little bit less in your place compared to your competitor next door or down the road that you've undercut by a few pence. But you actually have no idea if your competitor is making a profit. You could be copying the business strategy of a business that's about to go bust. Copying is crazy as you simply don't know what price they buy their ingredients for.

Thinking about the price points is an important part of setting a menu – as important as thinking about the dishes themselves. By thinking about price first you can come up with a menu that entices customers to spend and appears to be great value. By considering the entry price and top-end price and then splashing lots of other price points in between gives the opportunity for customers to spend low or high within their price bracket.

Thinking about price first gives great shape to your menu.

Entry-level main courses

Consider price in the light of the main target customer. Too low could cheapen the offer too much and put off a section of the market. Similarly, a high entry level price gives a clear message that the target market is exclusive and will appeal to that sector
What is the cheapest you are prepared to go? This will broaden your appeal as obviously a low entry level attracts customers. They may not eat the cheapest dish, but they've had the chance to do so if they had wanted

Top end

This is as important as entry level. People may be put off if you go too high but again the science of buying says that 20% of the clientele will want a more exclusive product, a chance to 'treat' themselves. You will be missing an opportunity if you do not give them that chance. Typically the most expensive dish will be steak or seafood.

The middle

Once you have picked your entry level and top end prices the next step is to create attractive price points in between. Don't make a lack of well-thought out price points a reason for customers not to spend their limited disposable income with you. Instead, help customers enjoy themselves more by increasing their spend per head at weekends when people are more prepared to treat themselves without putting off midweek diners who may want to pop out for a cheap bite.

Starters and desserts

Once settled on your mains price points, you need to decide on starters and dessert price points. Generally, having a couple of low-priced items will entice customers to eat an additional course and provide an opportunity for extra drinks sales.

Sharing plate starters and desserts are also a good way of tipping the balance in favour of an extra course.

As a rule of thumb - the entry starter price should be half the entry main and the top starter price shouldn't go much over the entry main course.

Food costs

Once you have your range of price points you will need to consider what food cost option each price point allows you and begin the task of matching menu items with appropriate costs.

While some flexibility is required to ensure common sense around cash margins as opposed to rigidly sticking to % margins (you can't bank a percentage) some thought also needs to be given to sales mix – there will be dishes that outsell everything else on your menu – and these are the ones you need to ensure you make maximum profit from.

Say, for example, you decide your steak should retail at £9.99 and you would like to achieve a GP of 60%. This means you will have £3.33 to spend on creating your steak dish – including garnish, chips, peas mushrooms and sauces. If you cannot source your steak at the quality you require at the price you need then you will have to think again.

Approaching menu construction in this way gives you opportunities to focus on the relationship between quality and price and its importance to your target market.

The sums:

1. Decide on your desired gross profit percentage   = **X**

2. Take the desired selling price and take off the VAT
   (the current VAT rate for food is 20% so you divide by 1.2) = **A**

3. **100 – X** (your desired gross profit percentage)   = **B**

4. **A ÷ 100 x B =**   Cost Price   **£**

Example:

1. Desired gross profit margin is 60%
2. Lasagne sells at £5.75 - take off the VAT £5.75 divided
   by 1.2 = £4.79 (A)
3. 100 – 60 = 40 (B)
4. (4.79 divided by 100 = 0.479) x 40 = £1.92 COST

If you know what something costs and you want to calculate the
retail price at a specific margin the calculation is as follows:
Cost price divided by (100 - your desired gross profit) x 100 x 1.2

Example:

- Cost price = £1.97
- Desired gross profit margin = 55%
- £1.97 divided by 45 (100 – 55 = 45) x 100 = £4.38
- £4.38 x 1.2 (VAT) = £5.25 (RETAIL PRICE)

The menu as a hard selling tool

Everyone reads the menu!

If you run a food outlet you will have a menu. Everyone who comes through your doors will read the menu if they want to eat. This makes your menu one of the most powerful marketing points in your business. Used intelligently, a menu can stimulate additional impulse high GP sales. Studies from the USA, including 'The Psychology of Menu Design: Reinvent Your "Silent Salesperson" to Increase Check Averages and Guest Loyalty' from Georgia State University suggest that increases in GP of up to 15% are possible - which will give the double whammy of making you more profit while simultaneously giving your customers an even better experience of visiting you. Keep that thought! We shall return to it within this chapter.

So why is it that very often the menu is given little effort and is treated simply as a list of dishes with prices?

A well-designed and well laid-out menu can dramatically affect your profitability by leading and influencing customers to make specific choices. The choices that you lead them to make should always reflect your most profitable dishes.

The first thing is to consider the text - people do not read in a constant, smooth progression across the text. Instead, our eyes dart around, remaining relatively stationary on one word or section of text and then darting on to the next part. This means that on any given page of writing there are areas where the eye naturally lingers.

The Gutenberg Rule identifies how the eye scans a piece of text.

1. **First visual area** – this is located in the top left and is where the eye starts on any piece of text

2. **Strong fallow area** - located in the top right – this area is

usually 'passed over' as the eye scans the text – by highlighting this area with a box, by using colour, or a different font or font size, one can encourage the eye to linger here and it becomes a sales placement 'hot spot'

3.   **Weak visual area** - located in the bottom left – this is not the 'hot spot' of top right but can be a useful sales location if the content is highlighted

4.   **Terminal area** - located in the bottom right – this is where the eye finishes its journey across the text and a natural place for it to linger

Z-Pattern Layout

As you would expect the Z-pattern layout follows the shape of the letter Z. Readers start in the top left, move horizontally to the top right and then diagonally to the bottom left before finishing with another horizontal movement to the bottom right.

As with Gutenberg, a menu designer would place the most important information along the pattern's path

If you have an extensive menu with text heavy content, it is worth noting that if you put dishes you want to sell more of emphasised in some way, such as boxing them or highlighting them in strong and weak areas, you will see an increase in sales of these dishes.

Important elements should be placed along the 'reading gravity path' and generally for a menu this means the dishes you place on the top two lines of text and at the bottom of the block of text will be selected more frequently than the items in the middle.

Designs that follow Gutenberg are said to be in harmony with natural reading gravity. With this in mind it is easy to see where one should place the dishes you want to sell most of on a menu page.

Even if you simply list your dishes without creating boxes and highlighted areas, you should always place these dishes on the top two lines and the bottom line as this follows the Z pattern.

Golden Triangle

The Z-pattern also leads to what's called a golden triangle pattern.

If you take the first horizontal and first diagonal movement and then close the shape you end up with a triangle whose right angle is the top left corner.

This triangular area at the top of the page will be the area most seen and the pattern suggests your most important information needs to be placed inside it. This means selecting your most profitable lines and placing them here. It is a great spot for putting 'additional sales' such as high GP side orders or drinks suggestions, as it is seldom missed by the reader.

Place high profit lines in menu 'hot spots' that follow the Z-pattern

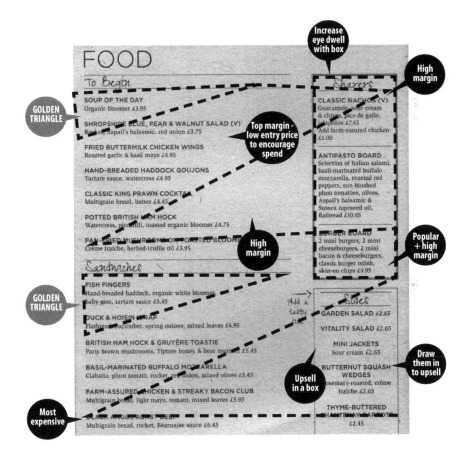

Increase eye dwell with box

High margin

FOOD

To Begin

GOLDEN TRIANGLE

SOUP OF THE DAY
Organic bloomer £3.95

SHROPSHIRE BLUE, PEAR & WALNUT SALAD (V)
Rocket, Aspall's balsamic, red onion £3.75

FRIED BUTTERMILK CHICKEN WINGS
Roasted garlic & basil mayo £4.95

HAND-BREADED HADDOCK GOUJONS
Tartare sauce, watercress £4.95

CLASSIC KING PRAWN COCKTAIL
Multigrain bread, butter £4.45

POTTED BRITISH HAM HOCK
Watercress, piccalilli, toasted organic bloomer £4.75

PAN-FRIED MUSHROOM ON TOASTED BLOOMER
Crème fraîche, herbed-truffle oil £3.95

Top margin - low entry price to encourage spend

High margin

Sandwiches

GOLDEN TRIANGLE

FISH FINGERS
Hand-breaded haddock, organic white bloomer, baby gem, tartare sauce £5.45

DUCK & HOISIN WRAP
Flatbread, cucumber, spring onions, mixed leaves £4.95

BRITISH HAM HOCK & GRUYÈRE TOASTIE
Paris brown mushrooms, Tiptree honey & beer mustard £5.45

BASIL-MARINATED BUFFALO MOZZARELLA
Ciabatta, plum tomato, rocket, red onion, mixed olives £5.45

FARM-ASSURED CHICKEN & STREAKY BACON CLUB
Multigrain bread, light mayo, tomato, mixed leaves £5.95

Most expensive

BLACK ANGUS RUMP STEAK
Multigrain bread, rocket, Béarnaise sauce £6.45

Sharers

CLASSIC NACHOS (V)
Guacamole, sour cream & chips, pico de gallo, jalapeños £7.45
Add farm-assured chicken £1.00

ANTIPASTO BOARD
Selection of Italian salami, basil-marinated buffalo mozzarella, roasted red peppers, sun-blushed plum tomatoes, olives, Aspall's balsamic & Sussex rapeseed oil, flatbread £10.95

BURGER BOARD
2 mini burgers, 2 mini cheeseburgers, 2 mini bacon & cheeseburgers, classic burger relish, skin-on chips £9.95

Popular + high margin

Sides

GARDEN SALAD £2.65

VITALITY SALAD £2.65

MINI JACKETS
Sour cream £2.65

BUTTERNUT SQUASH WEDGES
Rosemary-roasted, crème fraîche £2.65

THYME-BUTTERED NEW POTATOES
£2.45

Add a tasty side

Upsell in a box

Draw them in to upsell

67

Box-out corners of the menu to help the eye dwell there longer

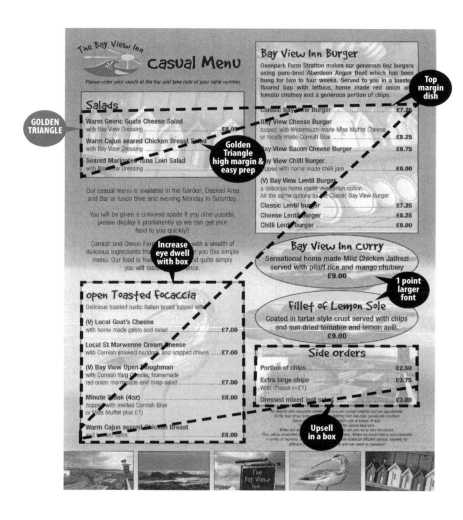

The Bay View Inn

Casual Menu

Please order your meals at the bar and take note of your table number.

Salads

GOLDEN TRIANGLE

Warm Gevric Goats Cheese Salad
with Bay View Dressing £8.00

Warm Cajun seared Chicken Breast Salad
with Bay View Dressing

Seared Marinated Tuna Loin Salad
with Bay View Dressing ....

Golden Triangle high margin & easy prep

Our casual menu is available in the Garden, Decked Area and Bar at lunch time and evening Monday to Saturday.

You will be given a coloured spade if you dine outside, please display it prominently so we can get your food to you quickly!!

Cornish and Devon Farms [**Increase eye dwell with box**] with a wealth of delicious ingredients from .... y you this simple menu. Our food is fres .... d quite simply you will tast .... nce.

Open Toasted Focaccia

Delicious toasted rustic Italian bread topped with

(V) Local Goat's Cheese
with home made pesto and salad £7.00

Local St Marwenne Cream Cheese
with Cornish smoked haddock and snipped chives £7.00

(V) Bay View Open Ploughman
with Cornish Yarg Cheese, homemade
red onion marmalade and crisp salad £7.00

Minute Steak (4oz) £8.00
(topped with melted Cornish Blue
or Miss Muffet plus £1)

Warm Cajun seared Chicken Breast
.... £8.00

Bay View Inn Burger

Oxenpark Farm Stratton makes our generous 6oz burgers using pure-bred Aberdeen Angus Beef which has been hung for two to four weeks. Served to you in a toasted floured bap with lettuce, home made red onion and tomato chutney and a generous portion of chips.

Top margin dish

Classic Bay View Burger £7.25

Bay View Cheese Burger
topped with Widemouth-made Miss Muffet Cheese
or locally made Cornish Blue £8.25

Bay View Bacon Cheese Burger £8.75

Bay View Chilli Burger
topped with home made chilli jam £8.00

(V) Bay View Lentil Burger
a delicious home made vegetarian option.
All the same options as the Classic Bay View Burger

Classic Lentil burger £7.25
Cheese Lentil burger £8.25
Chilli Lentil burger £8.00

Bay View Inn Curry

Sensational home made Mild Chicken Jalfrezi
served with pilaff rice and mango chutney
£9.00

1 point larger font

Fillet of Lemon Sole

Coated in tartar style crust served with chips
and sun dried tomatoe and lemon aoili.
£9.00

Side orders

Portion of chips £2.50

Extra large chips £3.75
With cheese (+£1)

Dressed mixed leaf salad £3.00

Upsell in a box

68

Quirky menu design following the Z pattern and Golden Triangle rules can drive customers to select the dishes you want them to buy

(Menu from: Bistrotheque, London)

Double Z Pattern ▶ ▶ ▶

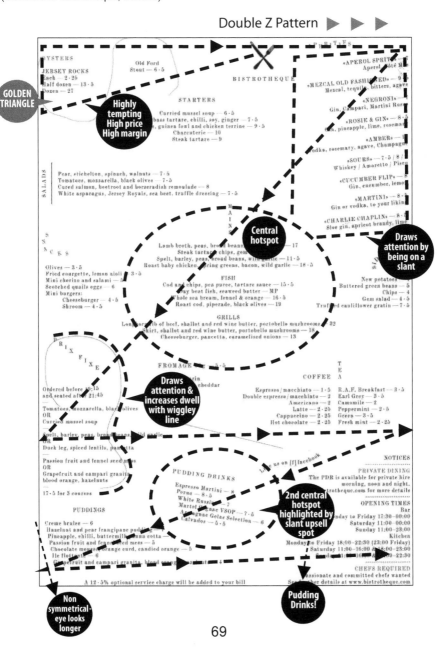

69

Choosing the right words

How you describe your food will influence your customers' perception of its flavour and perceived value for money.

Generally a well-described meal will be able to command a higher retail price.

Whether you choose Poncey or Plain Jane is up to you, the main thing is that it needs to be appropriate for your target customer group

'Battered cod and chips' is OK for the local cafe

'Freshly-caught cod, bursting with succulent flavour in crispy hand-made beer batter, served with melt-in-the-mouth crunchy, fluffy triple-cooked chips' may be better for a gastro pub/restaurant.

Research has shown using a *Provenance word in the description such as "Tamworth outdoor reared pork' gives you the edge when looking to command higher prices.

Professor Dan Jurafsky of Stamford University has studied the link between the wordiness of the menu and the price the restaurant charges. Jurafsky studied 6,500 menus and found the use of long words to describe a dish was a clear sign of a high price. His study showed that words such as 'exotic' and 'spicy' raise the price of a dish while vague gushing adjectives such as 'delicious', 'gourmet' and 'hearty' feature more in cheap menus.

Popular words

Crispy	Indulgent	Drizzled
Buttery	Succulent	Local
Hand-made	Roasted	Seared
Glazed	Pan-fried	Oven–roasted

Honey-seared	Butter-poached	Fresh
Market	Seasonal	Hand-picked
Caramelised	Gently	*Provenance
Home-made		

(Only use 'home-made' if it really is. If it isn't then it constitutes a breach of the Trade Descriptions Act in criminal law and you could be reported to the local Trading Standards department).

Be careful not to get too 'up yourself' with your language – there is a fine line between stimulating the taste buds with your descriptions and talking a load of pretentious twaddle.

Blocking

Laying your menu out in blocks rather than the traditional list will work well with the principles of eye-dwell described above. Try putting lower margin staples in the bottom left and drawing customer's eyes to the high margin items top right and bottom right.

Colour

Try using different colours to highlight specific dishes you want to sell – either as a background colour or by using a different coloured font in the descriptor. I personally stay away from red, which many associate with 'cheap'.

Fonts

Legible, legible, legible! I don't care how pretty this new elaborate font is that you've downloaded, if it's too ornate it will be hard to read (many of the ones that imitate handwriting are). If you've got a bit of mood lighting (or in 'real speak' partial darkness) going on in the premises you could potentially embarrass or annoy your customers.

Stick to one or two fonts only – one for the headers and one for the dishes and make the font size big enough to make it easy for your customers to read. Make it easy for your customer to spend more money with you – and have such a great time with you they recommend you to their friends!

Selecting one or two dishes that you want to promote and increasing the font size by just one or two points from the rest of the menu items will draw the customer's eye to that dish.

White Space

Space sells - don't be tempted to crowd too much written information onto a page, leave some spaces around blocks of text to make it easy to read. In many cases, less is more.

Personality

As an independent operator you have the chance to shine above the bland chain competition. Don't be frightened to inject some humour or personality into the menu. After the horse meat scandal in 2013 there was plenty of this type of comment on chalkboards:

'Our steaks have won awards but never won a race.'

Marketing

Given that everyone reads the menu, it can be a great place to promote other aspects of your business that customers may not realise. Things like private function catering, summer barbecues and special food nights. Possibly the best place to advertise menus, or anything else for that matter, is in the loos. Above the urinals and on the back of loo doors. You have a person's undivided attention for several minutes. While we're at it two hooks on the back of ladies loo doors are a good idea – one for coat, one for handbag.

Golden Rule No.8

Your menu is a sales tool. Design your menu specifically to increase sales of your most profitable lines. It makes your customers happy, it makes your kitchen happy, it makes your bank manager happy. A triple whammy!

Pricing tricks

Little ways to increase average spend

Supersize

Take the 'Big Ugly Burger' at the Farmers Boy Inn, Gloucestershire. Priced at a premium £25 the burger at this pub delivers on its promise of being supersize – weighing in at a total of nearly a kilo they are exclusive and in demand as they are only available on certain days in the month and are promoted as the 'Big Ugly Burger Challenge'. Anyone managing to finish one gets their photo in the pub's 'Hall of Fame.'

Everything seems to be bigger these days, including the nation's waistlines. Before joining the 'supersized' market consider the impact on sales: a supersized main course will probably lose you a sale of dessert and starter and so needs to have a price point that reflects this; then there will always be the customers who will order one supersize and share it between four. They may have spent twice the money if they'd had to select a dish each, so be careful it doesn't decrease your average spend per head.

However, if it's appropriate for your target clientele, done well, a 'supersize' menu option can be a great marketing tool creating a bit of a stir and a decent following with your customers. The Farmers Boy Inn has its own 'Big Ugly Burger' facebook page with people trying to get their photo published after completing the challenge.

Other supersizing options can include 'Feast for Two'; 'All You Can Eat'; 'The Belt Buster' and 'Go Mega' and generally one can charge a premium price for a supersize as customers' perceived value for money is generally as huge as the plateful in front of them.

Premiumisation

A colleague and I were out to lunch recently and both ordered the steak sandwich. The slightly inexperienced member of staff asked if we would like to upgrade to fillet steak – when we probed a bit about what we had already ordered we were left with the distinct impression that unless we took the upgrade our meal would be only one step up from shoe leather!

Making premiumisation work well involves effective implementation by staff. As a customer I want to be asked:

'Would you like to upgrade your juicy rump steak to an exquisitely marbled 28-day aged Aberdeen Angus Fillet?'

Rather than:

'You can spend a bit more on a fillet steak that's going to be more tender than the one you've ordered!'

Pareto's Law comes into play here (as indeed in most situations) and says that 20% of the population will choose a premium option if they are offered one. We so often get into the mindset which says everything must be priced lower than our competitors that we forget to give our customers an opportunity to spend a bit more.

Premiumisation is generally where a superior quality item is offered as an 'upgrade' to a standard item. This works really well with protein items on your menu such as fish (upgrade size of prawn); meat (upgrade rump to fillet steak) or other items such as upgrading a basket of bread to an 'Artisan Bread Board'.

However, premiumisation only works financially if you have carefully costed your premium version of your dish.

Here's an example using a wholesale price to you:

A rump steak costs £2.50

A fillet steak costs £3.75

The rest of the dish (garnish and fries) costs £1.00

The retail price of the rump is £10.95 (£9.13 ex VAT) and the GP is £5.62.

By offering to upgrade to a fillet steak for an extra £4 to £14.95 (£12.45 ex VAT) you increase this Gross Profit to £7.70. So, you've gained another £2.08 against a cost of only £1.25 meaning you have more cash in your till and the customer has treated themselves to a higher price meal they would not normally have selected.

Build a Dish

This is a 21st Century invention, which has a great deal of customer appeal and makes a lot of sense with regard to price points and profit.

'Build a dish' works by offering a basic, but perfectly pleasant and acceptable dish (particularly good in a casual dining environment) at a low price point, but allowing people to 'customise' it to their own taste adding their own toppings and extras.

For example you could invite people to 'Build your own burger or hot dog' by adding another burger or dog for £1.50, and adding toppings at 95p each including: cheese, coleslaw, jalepenos, bacon, egg, salad etc.

This makes commercial sense too. Take this 'build a pizza' example:

Margherita sells for £4 retail and cost £1.10 with GP on basic dish at 67%

Customers are able to add their own choice of toppings for 95p each:

Mozarella at a low wholesale cost of 30p
Peppers at a low wholesale cost of 20p
Pepperoni at a low wholesale cost of 25p
Mushrooms at a low wholesale cost of 13p
Jalapenos at a low wholesale cost of 12p

If someone builds a pizza with all five toppings (5 x 95p) you will retail it for £8.75 at a cost of £2.10 giving you 71% GP on the higher spend per head (SPH).

Each 'extra' has a low food cost value and even when sold as an extra at a modest price, say, between 50p and £1 can add 70-80% in GP for each item.

There will always be the 20% that choose the basic unbuilt dish (good old Pareto again) and that means your GP % may well be lower on these dishes, although it shouldn't be if you have costed the basic dish accurately. However, if you sell the deal well and have well-trained persuasive staff who enjoy the customer interaction, fun and challenge of upselling, the 80% that build their own will end up choosing more than they would have done if left to their own devices. And they'll consequently enjoy themselves more – and come back to spend more of their money with you.

There is also a lovely 'theatre' attached to letting customers get involved in designing what they are eating which when done well creates another dimension to customer engagement and loyalty.

Top Tip

It's worth mentioning that if you are going to use this technique on your menu there is a point beyond which your customers will not want to go; far from creating fun and loyalty you could invite derision and dissatisfaction. Just think of the budget airlines' reputation where people really hate being charged for the extras that are essential (luggage, going for a wee). The secret is to get the balance right – you have been warned!

Golden Rule No.9

A brilliant and well balanced menu is central to your business. Use your imagination to create something fun and interesting for the customers and strategically profitable for you.

More Profit Vampires that will suck your margins

Golden Rule No 7 states that guessing is not an option – and yet it is really quite staggering, considering the high operational costs of running a restaurant, how many people leave this one core and essential aspect of their operation to chance. It is shocking how many people try to run a profitable food business by guessing costs and not having an accurate dish specification to work to.

No.9 Guessing your cost price

Your chef may assure you his method of taking the protein cost, adding 50p and multiplying by 3.5 will deliver 'near enough' profit. The fact is that whenever these guestimates are subsequently accurately costed, an uplift in profit is guaranteed – usually in excess of 5%. Over the course of the year that's a huge impact.

One of the fundamentals of any retail business is to know exactly what something costs you before you re-sell it

But as we've seen earlier in this chapter, with food this isn't always as straightforward as it seems, particularly if you make all or some of your menu from scratch, or use raw ingredients rather than bought in prepared food. However, that's still no excuse to revert to guesswork, it will cost you dearly if you do.

Think about it:

If you were a publican would you ever consider selling all your pints of beer in unmeasured glassware relying on guesswork for how much to serve?

No, of course not, for one thing to do so would it breech trading standards regulations, but that aside, a keg of lager contains 88 pints and you measure each one accurately to ensure you sell all

88. If a keg costs you £100 that means each pint has a cost of £1.14. If you only get 85 pints from a keg each one will cost you £1.18 – you will lose 4p profit on every one sold.

If you were a sweet shop would you ever consider buying a case of sweets and letting the customers pick and mix without a set of scales?

If you were a petrol station would you serve customers fuel without a calibrated pump to measure volume?

So why do so many operators think it's ok to guess their food costs? It's bonkers!

Profit Vampire

No.10 Garnish

Over-garnishing food with unnecessary herbs and salad.

How you garnish your food matters. If you find the majority ends up left on the plate and ultimately in the bin, the waste isn't just the cost of the product (lettuce is the biggest offender). Consider also the man hours used over the year to prepare the garnish - washing it, chopping it and assembling it - as well as the power used to refrigerate it. Expensive ingredients such as fancy frilly lettuce and micro herbs have a limited lifespan so if you over-order there will be even more in the bin.

Top Tip

Reduce your reliance on salad as a garnish. Not only is it an expensive option, which your customers don't actually order (if they'd wanted a side salad – they'd have ordered one right?), but you'll be paying to have your commercial waste collected from site – containing all that uneaten salad garnish – the more you fill the bins the more you'll be paying. The Sustainable Restaurant Association estimates an average restaurant wastes over £17,000 of food a year!

Creating an 'Oh Wow!' effect when you set a dish down on the table doesn't have to rely on expensive crockery but if you can create it, it does mean higher perceived value by your customer which can command a higher price. All it takes is a bit of imagination - The Treby Arms in Sparkwell, Devon, serves Carrot Cake dessert in a flowerpot with chocolate soil and candied carrots garnish!

Real life example of Profit Vampires 10 and 11 at work:

I thought you might like to hear about Sharon. Sharon ran a great pub in Bath offering food, drink, curry and steak nights, karaoke and live music - nothing fancy, but good traditional British pub classics such as Paninis, Jackets, Fish and Chips, Steak, Burgers and Lasagne. When Sharon first started speccing out her dishes she focused on them one at a time, just making small, but highly effective, tweaks. Take her Paninis for example, which she served with a salad garnish (that cost her 31p, usually went un-eaten and ended up in the bin).

I suggested that Sharon ditch the garnish and replace it with a 180g portion of chips (at a cost to her of 14p), served in a small basket on a nicer plate to both look good and ensure strict portion control. Instead of charging £4.45 per sandwich she upped it to £4.95 as customer perception of the dish as representing good value for money increased with the addition of the chips and better tableware. Figures for the following quarter showed an average 8% increase in GP for her sandwich offer which translated to £149.64 profit or £598.56 projected profit for the whole year. That's nearly £600 for very little effort.

She continued this theme including implementing better buying practices from the kitchen team without sacrificing quality (bacon was 6p a rasher cheaper from supplier number two but the kitchen team were always running out so they repeatedly bought from supplier number one because it was convenient to them).

From just five lines that account for only 6% of her volume sales, another £600 was added to her bottom line this year. These are REAL figures. See below how those tiny changes that you're tempted to I-G-N-O-R-E soon add up.

PANINI VARIETY	13 Week Sales	Increase in GP after changes	Additional Profit ££ in 13 weeks
Bacon & Mushroom	£618.20	+ 10%	£61.82
Tomato and Mozz	£283.87	+7%	£19.87
Tuna Melt	£257.46	+5%	£12.87
Cheddar & Chutney	£118.04	+10%	£11.80
BBQ Chicken	£540.98	+8%	£43.28
Extra annual bottom line profit from 6% of menu sales mix	**£598.56 annually**		

In addition Sharon confided that one of the biggest improvements to her profitability had come from putting some proper purchasing systems in place. The staff were constantly running out of staples like bacon and just running to the local convenience store where they paid three times the price for it!

No.12 Not having a dish spec

One of the single biggest causes of lost profit is not having a clearly defined, fully costed and up-to-date list of ingredients and component recipes to work to.

Food retail is no different to any other retail and means one should adhere to the fundamental rule of business which is to know exactly what every component that makes up each meal is, down to the last gram, and know the cost price for every recipe and every dish.

Without an accurate dish specification how can you hold your kitchen staff accountable for what goes out on a plate?

As I said right at the start of this book, the profit is there for the taking in every commercial kitchen; it is, however, hard work to find the little pockets of pennies that soon mount up into thousands of pounds.

Take this example of how small discrepancies can have a big impact on bottom-line profit. If every day everything is perfectly measured, cooked and served, then the bottom line is that you would be ££££s better off than when chef and his team are only a little slapdash.

The problem for you is that the amount of sub-recipes within your menu (even a basic menu with a lot of bought-in dishes will have maybe 25 or so sub-recipes that they make from scratch – things like sauces, gravies and batched items like stews and batter). That's why having an accurate recipe or dish specification as a template to refer to, is vital.

Is chef having a bad day?

Not sticking to a dish specification can almost halve your profit.
Look what happens when your chef is having a bad day...

Chef has a **GOOD DAY**		Chef has a **BAD DAY**	
The perfect burger Retails £5.95		The not so perfect burger Retails £5.95	
1 floured bap	11p	I ciabatta - *we forgot to order floured baps*	26p
6oz home-made beef burger patty	36p	8oz home-made beef burger patty – *can't find the burger ring to measure*	48p
3 little gem lettuce leaves	15p	I little gem lettuce – *new girl on garnish*	50p
2 slices of beef tomato	24p	2 slices of beef tomato	24p
1 slice of red onion	4p	I slice red onion - *ran out had to get some from the corner shop and pay more*	10p
1 tablespoon of mayonnaise	15p	2 tablespoons of mayonnaise- *forgot how much it should be*	30p
1 x 2oz slice cheddar cheese	26p	2 slices of Emmental - *couldn't find the Cheddar this'll do – it's got holes in so put in extra*	78p
	£1.31		**£2.66**
Gross Profit	71%	Gross Profit	46%
Sell 10 a day		Sell 10 a day	
Weekly GP	£255.50	Weekly GP	£161.00
Annual GP	£13,286.00	Annual GP	£8,372.00

£4,914.00 more profit per year on just one menu line when chef is having a good day!

81

This is where CaterCost can really help.

Unlike spreadsheets, sub-recipes flow through the whole system as a fully costed commodity, with price increases – enter one and they too flow through the system.

When creating a sub-recipe the profitability can be tweaked by accurately defining a portion - 125 grams rather than 130 grams will unlock hundreds of pounds of profit if it's a big seller – your customers won't know the difference as long as you are providing value for money; your profits on the other hand will!

Visit www.CaterCost.com to see for yourself or take the free trial

Dish specification

The value of creating dish specifications are many – you can use them as a management tool and know that even if chef gets hit by a bus (heaven forbid) you have the formulas to carry on as normal. For portion control a dish spec is invaluable..

But more than that it gives you a control mechanism to cover the problem of that staff member who has done something in the same way – day-in day-out for years but suddenly decides – 'today I'm going to do it differently.' This happens in reality – God knows why! The net effect if today's customers get twice as much garnish is that you get half the profit!

The truth is, if you want to be in a position to have that tricky conversation about portions or ingredients with any team member – you'd better have a detailed dish spec in place.

An estimated 98% of independent food operators don't, so they're on a hiding to nothing. How can you say there are too many chips on that plate if you haven't determined exactly how many SHOULD be on it.

Defining your dish specification is genuinely the first step to creating a profitable and well-managed food offer.

Take Andy from the White Hart:

Andy's restaurant offer was based on high quality produce with every item freshly-prepared and cooked.

Andy's stock results showed a food GP% of 65% - his chef assured him that he had costed dishes in his head and should be getting 70%. Without an accurate dish specification as a benchmark there was no logical way to investigate what was going on as the answer could lie in one or more of several areas:

- *Over-portioning*
- *Poor buying practices*
- *Till errors*
- *Theft*
- *Wastage*
- *Staff food*

Andy felt that it may be his buffet menu that was to blame for his low GP but accurately speccing it out revealed he was looking in the wrong place - buffets showed a GP well above his desired 72%. The point is that until he started to accurately analyse his actual costs and portions he was merely guessing where things were going wrong.

Once an accurate dish spec and individual dish margin is identified it is possible to identify exactly the difference between what happens in theory and in practice, as this is often the missing link

Once an accurate dish spec is in place and used in conjunction with menu item sales – an accurate sales mix figure can be measured – it may be that a top-seller with low GP is pulling down the overall GP

See Recipe and Dish Costing templates in Chapter 7.

Shrinkage

Shrinkage occurs in many guises – the cooking process may reduce the yield from certain products such as roast meats, preparation will reduce the usable amount of products – peelings, trimming, filleting all mean that the final portion may have a much higher cost per kilo than the buying price.

This should always be accounted for in food costings. For example, home-made triple-cooked chips may seem a much cheaper alternative to prepared bought-in chips – but they can lose as much as 70% of their weight in the peeling, pre-cooking and final cooking process – see Chapter 4 for more detail.

Menu engineering

Once you understand the individual profit of every dish on your menu you can really play around with where you place items on the menu – see Chapter 3.

No.13 Not using menu hotspots

Not positioning your most profitable lines in the best spot on the menu.
Dishes that you want to sell more of (most profitable, easiest to prepare, short-dated) should always be placed on the first or second line of a block of text or as the last item at the bottom. These are the three lines that will sell more dishes. Putting a dish in a box, giving an imaginative headline, slightly larger font or at the centre menu page or top right hand side will ensure greater sales.

No.14 Not scrutinising supplier prices

Be careful of suppliers who give you 'top twenty' super discount prices yet inflate some other basic prices to well above market price.

No.15 Using high cost ingredients

Dishes using a high cost ingredient (fillet steak, lobster, prawns) will generally deliver a lower margin. Make sure the cash margin you achieve for these is at the top end in contributing to your profits.

Top Tip

I recently heard about the Old Homestead Steakhouse, a Manhattan restaurant (motto: 'Specializing in the Four Foodgroups – Beef, Beef, Beef and Beef!') that sold out in hours when they launched authentic Kobe beef from Wagyu cattle at the £ equivalent price of

£235! Romping home at a staggering cost of £120 per kilo, and serving a 10oz portion with fries and sides, the dish cost came to just over £46 and delivered a 75% margin. What can we learn from this (other than there are a lot of rich Americans)? It strikes me that there are two things at play here – understanding your target market and the prices they are prepared to pay, and not compromising your margins to accommodate dish ingredient prices.

So many times we are tempted to squeeze our margins because we want to offer the sort of quality that should have a high price tag attached.

Kobe facts:

- Authentic Kobe must be pure-bred Tajima calf born in Hyōgo Prefecture
- Farm fed only from grains and water from Hyōgo Prefecture
- Castrated bull or virgin cow, to purify the beef
- Processed at slaughterhouses in Kobe, Nishinomiya, Sanda, Kakogawa and Himeji in Hyōgo Prefecture only
- Marbling ratio, called BMS, of level 6 and above
- Meat Quality Score of 4 or 5
- Gross weight of beef from one animal is 470kg or less

A few more Profit Vampires

No.16 Emergency purchasing

Beware dashing to the supermarket, or worse still the convenience store, on a regular basis because you have run out of a food line item. Buying more expensive substitutes on out of stocks, whether deliberate or not, is the quickest way to erode your precious margins. Introduce systems to ensure you order from approved suppliers with negotiated prices. Keep a check on stock location and rotation to avoid ordering something already in stock.

No.17 Plate size

Using a plate that doesn't have a rim will tempt you to put a bigger portion on the plate to fill it. A rimmed plate will frame your food beautifully and in your customers eyes will add perceived value compared to a smaller rimless plate. Pasta bowls with rims for 'runny' dishes such as stews will ensure better presentation and strict portion control.

No.18 Bad storage

Desserts are prone to this profit vampire in particular and can result in the 'last slice' always being a bit too bashed around to actually sell. Ensure everything in the fridge is covered and items aren't stacked on top of each other. Rotate stock to ensure older items aren't lurking at the back of the fridge.

Golden Rule No.10

The devil is in the detail. Little tweaks to your food presentation translate into big differences in food profit and keep the Profit Vampires away.

4 Attention to detail

It's all about the food...

...or the equipment?

Falling into the seductive trap (as I have done) to introduce a special food night, such as Fish & Chip Friday, which was hugely popular with customers but totally ineffectual as a sustainable marketing plan. My one minute, cheap and cheerful table top fryer dropped temperature like a stone every time I placed a frozen fish in it, and only had room for one portion of chips at a time. Customers on that first F&C night were waiting for too long – which meant the take on the bar was great as people supped while they waited but not a long-term plan as repeat sales the following Friday amounted to nothing.

On a gourmet club evening we decided to go French – I think we'd just beaten them at rugby or some such similar triumph worth celebrating. The menu was lavish and we were fully-booked. A financial triumph until I realised I had forked out most of the profits on special holders and pickers for eating the snail course!

If you have an unlimited budget, then lucky you, you have a blank canvas and can craft the menu of your dreams safe in the knowledge that you are able to create a fully functioning kitchen to prepare and serve every dish.

If there is a limit on your investment cash it becomes a compromise between being all about the food and all about the equipment. When designing your menu you really need to make sure you have the kit, the right tools to deliver the menu efficiently. If you don't you will be storing up problems for when you're busy by being unable to cook and serve the food efficiently resulting in keeping your customers waiting, or wasting food (burning, shrinking, drying out) that's not been cooked with the right equipment.

Before you get carried away with the menu ask yourself 'what will we need to use to execute it efficiently'?

1. **Storage** - can we store all the produce needed for these dishes?

2. **Preparation** - do we have all the equipment needed to prepare these dishes?

3. **Cooking** - do we have all the equipment to cook these dishes and where necessary reheat these dishes?

4. **Service** - do we have all the equipment we need to serve these dishes?

I know it sounds obvious but it's amazing how these things can get overlooked when you're new! Kitchen equipment (apart from wages, business rates, rent, insurance and utility costs) is one of the single biggest drains on your capital. It's like that baby starling with an ever open mouth squeaking 'feed me' except it's not worms that are required – it's twenty pound notes – and lots of them.

Let's be quite clear, pretty much all of the equipment you bought with the inventory will be knackered, held together with Sellotape in some cases. And unless you are very lucky there will be no MOT certificate or proof of regular servicing and maintenance on items like stoves, microwaves, fryers, fridges and freezers. You will have a PAT Test certificate because it's law, which in itself is no guarantee that the equipment is working, just that it's not dangerous, and that's all.

If you haven't already signed the deal, be prepared to be a 'pain-in-the-bum' to the vendor and road test every bit of kit you are purchasing with the inventory. If it doesn't work make sure it appears as zero value.

If you've already bought then you may have already learned the hard way and filled a skip or two with items that looked shiny, but ended up as useless as a chocolate teapot.

You also need to familiarise yourself with 'Sod's Law'

Sod's Law means the LPG gas will never run out on a Monday (we had two places on LPG and this was a regular occurrence and particularly traumatic as we cooked on gas and our fryers were gas).

On a Monday, a relatively quiet day, if you ran out of gas you'd get through service somehow, a bit stressy – but hey it's a quiet day and you have five full working days to get emergency gas supplies. But Sod's Law dictates that will never happen. Gas will always run out at 6.30pm on a Saturday night when you have a fully-booked restaurant and the prospect of a packed Sunday lunch ahead, with no hope of getting the chaps on the emergency number to pick up.

Sod's Law in Action (or freezers on fire at Christmas)

With our 70 cover restaurant fully-booked one Christmas, and in anticipation of the Christmas week deliveries arriving, I asked husband Clive to defrost a freezer, which he did - with a blow torch. This flame-thrower, balanced on a box of 48 dozen paper napkins, was aimed at the iced-up interior. What genius! As events panned out, and in need of the loo, he popped off for a couple of minutes and the inevitable happened, the blow torch toppled and the result was a rapidly spreading fire in the food store (ah those napkins). I can't remember how many freezers full of prepped Christmas stock we lost, or how hard it made it to operate as normal – I think I have blanked the pain from my mind - all I know was that this would only ever happen at the busiest week of the year, any other time that blowtorch would have stayed upright! That's the Law of Sod!

Whether it's fridges breaking, grills, fryers or microwaves blowing-up, Sod's Law insists they are all pre-programmed in the factory to never break down until it causes maximum nuisance.

Unless you have unlimited capital for equipment, you will need to bear in mind a 'work with what we've got' mentality when designing your menu.

Sometimes it's worth the investment. The 'fresh local ingredients' menu I knew would seduce my target customers was only really viable once I stumped up a lot of cash for a walk-in fridge the size of the Isle of Wight. Other times it's worth 'making do' with cheap and cheerful.

Some bits of kit are worth spending on if you're able: a decent hob, fryer, Rationale or microwave will all take a bashing and need to be robust enough not to break down every five minutes.

Head Chef Chris Adey taught me this:

We had developed an Aberdeen Angus 28-day aged burger at our Cornish place (long before the Gourmet Burger became mainstream. Gosh, weren't we trailblazers!) The trouble was they were so popular our griddle wasn't big enough to cope. Drooling over the glossy brochures of expensive bits of kit, Chris suggested we go for the cheapest option. A cheap griddle can cost under £200 - we were planning on selling 10,000 burgers in the first year (27 a day). His logic was if it breaks in the first year (we really did put it through its paces) it's covered by warranty (replacement or repair) and if it lasts a second year that's a bonus. When it finally conks out we buy a new one; effectively treating the griddle as a disposable cost. What we did was add 2p a burger onto our dish cost to factor in buying a replacement.

 Golden Rule No.11

Beware of Sod's Law – if anything can possibly go wrong with kitchen equipment it will and it will happen at a time designed to cause maximum inconvenience, difficulty and stress.

Food makes you fat and allergic

You need to know this

Is it horse - do customers know what's in their food?
Do customers really want to know what's in their food?

Before the 2012 horse meat scandal, we British didn't really know what was in much of our food - and neither, it seemed, did half the food suppliers. And when we found out the truth - for example, that some beef lasagne, from a trusted, award-winning supermarket chain, contained horse meat the entire nation was shocked.

The trend toward transparency in clearly stating all ingredients in processed food - and food served by the catering industry - was growing anyway, but the horse meat scandal has increased the focus of the public and Government. It has brought about a sea-change in Britons' attitude to what's on their plates. Before the scandal, customers sort of trusted the food supply chain. They don't now.

So, to answer the question: do customers really want to know what's in their food?

The answer is 'yes'. They damned well do and the more information, the better.

And the Government is in tune with the British people here.

Back in 2011, before the scandal, the Government had already introduced a voluntary code that urged businesses providing 'out of home dining,' such as pubs, cafes, restaurants and fast-food outlets, to give customers details about the calories and salt content of the food they serve. The chains have been publishing this information from day one, and consumers are getting used to being able to see exactly what's in their menu choices.

In addition, the focus has now shifted to allergens, that is, foods which contain a chemical that induces an allergic reaction in someone who eats it. Allergic reactions to food can sometimes cause serious illness and death.

Labelling laws for the food service industry changed in December 2014, meaning all operators or suppliers offering food have to provide allergy information about their menu The legislation means that specific food allergens listed within the EU regulation FIR 1169/2011, including peanuts and gluten, must be highlighted.

This legislation means that stating: 'We cannot guarantee our dishes don't contain an allergenic food ingredient' is not an option. Food operators are obliged to provide clear information about the food allergens contained in their dishes.

These allergens need to be highlighted on menus, packaging, and displays. Verbal information can be given by the staff, however, back-up written confirmation of the details will be required and can be requested by customers at any time. If information is given verbally there is a requirement for 'signpost' statements to inform customers.

What are the allergens involved?

The 14 allergens that food businesses and venues will need to declare to customers are:

1. **Cereals which contain gluten** - protein found in wheat and other cereal grains including barley, oats, rye and spelt. These are the main cereals but the onus is on, you, the operator to personally check with suppliers whether their products contain gluten). The grain of origin must be identified and disclosed on the label.

2. **Crustaceans** - such as shrimp, prawn, crab, crayfish, lobster. Often these are found as a hidden ingredient in ethnic products and prepared sauces

3. **Molluscs** - such as oysters, snails, scallops, mussels and clams.

4. **Fish** - including any fresh water or sea fish. Things like Worcestershire Sauce contain fish, as an ingredient listed on the label is 'anchovy'

5. **Peanuts** - often known as beer nuts or monkey nuts.

6. **Lupin** - seeds crushed to make flour or eaten whole, often used in European baked products

7. **Nuts** - tree nuts such as walnuts, hazelnuts, almonds etc. The nut of origin must be disclosed on the label

8. **Soya or soy** - often seen on labels as 'textured vegetable protein'

9. **Eggs** - from birds such as hen, duck, goose

10. **Milk** – any mammalian milk

11. **Celery** – including celeriac and celery salt (used in stocks and often present in every day staples such as ketchup)

12. **Mustard** – seeds and powder

13. **Sesame** – sometimes referred to as 'gingelly 'or 'benne'.

14. **Sulphur-dioxide** - used as a preservative in wines, beer and fruit, sometimes referred to as sulphites.

It doesn't matter if it's real or not.

The Anaphylactic Society (a consumer group campaigning, among other topics, for clearer understanding of what's in our food) reckons that 22% of the population believe they have some kind of food allergy. Whether these are genuine medically diagnosed allergies or not, it really doesn't matter – if someone thinks they are allergic to a specific food group, they will avoid eating that food group!

The food service industry should certainly listen as this represents nearly a quarter of the UK's potential diners.

What can you do?

This sounds quite daunting; especially for smaller independent outlets, but many businesses have procedures in place and some quite small adjustments will be enough as long as your staff know what allergens are in the food they're serving.

The truth is, it's not that scary a proposition. You don't have to rejig your entire menu to make everything allergy-friendly. If you offer just a handful of items on a menu that exclude some of the 14 allergens then you can market that successfully. Preparing the ingredients and preventing cross-contamination is just an extension of the food preparation process you should already have in place.

Allergy vs Intolerance

It's worth mentioning the difference between a food allergy and food intolerance here. A food allergy is a rapid and potentially serious response to a food by your immune system. It can trigger classic allergy symptoms such as a rash, wheezing and itching.
Food intolerances are more common than food allergies and the symptoms tend to come on more slowly, often many hours after eating the problem food. Typical symptoms include bloating and stomach cramps. It's possible to be intolerant to several different foods. This can make it difficult to identify which foods are causing the problem.

Is it worth it?

Yes. Very well worth it. The argument that the one person with an allergy (or who thinks they have an allergy) or an intolerance in a group of diners decides where the others are eating is very strong, so there is potentially a decent return on any investment in your research and labelling.

As the number of customers with dietary requirements grows, the business that doesn't cater for those requirements could see a downturn in trade and this is partly being driven by allergy-friendly review websites. The Anaphylaxis Campaign has developed a review directory for members to share eating-out experiences called

'Tried and Trusted'. Members input reviews of the best, and worst, restaurants, pubs and hotels with regards to their allergy understanding. You've only got to think of TripAdvisor to realise these review sites can be very influential indeed. Your customers have the choice

You may have your own views about calorie and nutritional data labelling, but ultimately your customers will determine this issue. If they are increasingly used to being able to get food content details in restaurants, coffee shops and casual dining, you may find they'll start to avoid your establishment if you are unable to provide this.

Put simply, if you won't tell them what's in your food, they won't trust you.

Increasingly, outlets are cashing in by marketing and offering 'low fat' or 'low calorie' options for increasingly discerning customers – some professional caterers used to privately refer to these people as 'fussy' or 'faddish' - but in a more customer-focused, more professional and skilled industry, we've moved on from such old fashioned views.

And we need to move on: an estimated one in three women and one in five men in Britain are on a diet at any given time. So, by finding a section on your menu that will not blow their diet when they eat out with friends is a great business-driver, particularly if you are a casual dining outlet.

But why not turn this into a positive? If you can develop a tasty treat (a burger perhaps) that will astound your customers with how nutritionally sound it is - that's a big unique selling point for your business which you can market and develop with other dishes.

Knowing your target customer and what's important to them will help you decide if this is right for your place.

However you only have to look at what's been happening in the USA to get a glimpse of what might be in store for the UK. There are 155 million obese people in the USA.

Obesity figures in the USA are constantly shifting – upwards. According to a 2011 report by the American Heart Association (AHA) surveying Americans aged 20 and older, 154.7 million (79.9

million men. - 74.8 million women) were overweight or obese (BMI of 25.0 and higher).

The total cost related to the current obesity epidemic in the US is estimated to be $254 billion ($208 billion in lost productivity secondary to premature morbidity and mortality and $46 billion in direct medical costs). The AHA is predicting total healthcare costs attributable to obesity will reach $861 to $957 billion by 2030, which would account for 16% to 18% of US health expenditure.

Nutritional data on food is a hot potato in this political arena.

The US government, recognising that many Americans make fewer nutritionally sound food choices when eating out than when eating food prepared at home, introduced compulsory food labelling in chain restaurants (20+ sites) in 2011, believing one reason for the poorer nutritional quality of restaurant choices may be lack of information. When shopping at food stores, consumers can compare packaged food items by their nutritional content, such as calories, saturated fat, and salt. When dining out, such comparisons were difficult.

With obesity rates in the UK still rising and the UK being crowned the 'fattest country in Europe in 2013', it would be no surprise to see the voluntary code made mandatory – in fact policy is being shaped to do just this as I write!

While calculating the nutritional content of made-from-scratch dishes may seem daunting for the independent operator, cloud technology helps with one system, CaterCost, specifically designed to overcome the problem in a user-friendly and simple way. Check out www.CaterCost.com and try for yourself on our free trial.

If you ask your chef whether this is a good idea, nine times out of 10 he or she won't think it is because it will mean more work for them and they will have to do something differently.

The point you need to consider is simple: 'Is your chef your customer?' No, he/she isn't. But if she or he are professionals, they should be as tuned-in to current trends as you. Every business has to evolve with its market to stay prosperous. If you don't evolve, you'll get left behind. Simple.

Your entire kitchen staff, as well as front-of-house, have to know you are running a business that needs to respond to trends and seize every trading and marketing opportunity to maximise your income. If you don't, your competition just might pinch the health-conscious trade from under your nose – and they'll be without a job.

Put simply – however much, or little, you know about commercial kitchens, your chef is your employee and you must be in control, not them. You will need to 'manage' their creativity and balance it with your commercial knowledge, particularly if they are anti disclosing nutritional content.

 Golden Rule No.12

>   **Customers want to know what's in their food. If you don't give them an option to select low calorie and allergen free menu items, you're effectively turning your back on a quarter of the UK's population.**

Your signature dish

Do just one thing...really, really well!

Often on a menu there will be one dish that is 'super special' and associated in the minds of the customer with that outlet, and that outlet alone.

- Snail Porridge at the Fat Duck
- Tea at the Ritz
- Big Mac at McDonalds

At any level it is possible to create one dish that will define the perceived quality of your entire menu, create loyalty from your customers and set you apart from other similar outlets in your sector.

At the level of haute cuisine a 'signature dish' is a recipe that identifies an individual chef. Ideally it should be unique and allow an informed 'gastronome' to name the chef in a blind tasting. That's not to say any outlet can't have similar. At our Cornish pub the signature dish was the Bay View Burger made with locally sourced ingredients. We sold around £80k of these annually!

By doing one dish really, really well with really good quality ingredients, consistently, you start the stuff of legends – you need to create a signature dish and become famous for it. Every successful outlet I've run has had its signature dish.

You want a hundred people to tell their friends (who haven't spent money at your outlet before). 'Have you seen the House Burger at the X? It's awesome. To die-for.' And let's build on this - if you and your kitchen team work hard to develop a dish that's got the Wow! factor, it's damned tasty and appealing to females as well as males - and IS NUTRITIONALLY healthy - how can you fail to build a name for yourself.

The best - and most inexpensive - form of marketing is customer recommendation. Get it right, and you'll have hundreds of delighted customers busy telling their friends how brilliant you are.

Rules for creating a signature dish

1. **Keep it simple** - don't overcomplicate it. Remember, if it's successful your kitchen will be turning them out by the hundred

2. **Consistency is key** - if you are going to become renowned for an amazing dish, it had better be amazing time after time. The last thing you want is a customer to bring friends especially to try this astounding dish and find it presented differently, with a different topping or a wee bit smaller

3. **Create theatre around it** - theatre can be created through supersizing or 'Wow' presentation such as served sizzling, cooked at the table or stacked high on the plate

4. **Name** - think 'Reggae Reggae' sauce, it's a pretty similar sauce to loads of hot chilli sauces on the market but the name crowns it king. It stands out. Get your staff to create a stand-out name!

5. **Practical** - sometimes a signature dish is created as a way of using up leftovers

In the early days we created a lunch signature, quite by accident really! It was a simple toastie created to use up yesterday's bloomer bread. We cut ultra-thick slices and topped with melted cheese and bits that were always available in the kitchen – ham, mushroom, onions or pepper. It was really simple and cost-effective but customers loved this big plate of comfort food. It made us really good margin too!

6. **Let it evolve** - sometimes sales patterns will determine what your signature dish should be. Your job is to identify the dish your customers are buying most and elevate it to legendary status

7. **Quality** - it's worth spending a bit extra to 'over-deliver' on the quality and taste of your signature dish, once it is established as the most desired item on the menu you will be able to achieve premium price

8. **Unique recipe** - create interest with 'mystery' and exclusivity. 'Our unique recipe' intrigues diners and makes this item stand out from the rest

9. **Create a story around the dish** - bring your dish to life by talking about where ingredients come from. By telling your customers the effort you go to ensure perfection, you will get them to understand you really care about your food. Don't worry, they won't be bored by it and you can use the story in your marketing

A hugely successful Midlands pub introduced an old-fashioned Carvery for Sunday Lunch which had the 'Wow Factor' - and they hugely impress their customers with the high quality and integrity of their meat by displaying the identity tags of the actual animal they were serving - along with photographs of the farmers in the fields who raised it. Customers would drive past dozens of other pubs and restaurants serving Sunday lunch to spend their money at this business. They had got it right and enjoyed premium pricing, which customers were delighted to pay.

Another pub, with a tiny cubby hole for a commercial kitchen, has won a huge local reputation for its monster beef, pork and chicken rolls which are available from 5.30pm. Locals going home from work queue up for this legendary treat that is simple to produce and with a high GP. Oh, and they stay and have a drink too.

Top Tip

Some outlets lend themselves to doing just one thing and doing it really well. My favourite pub in Dorset proudly announces that it sells two dishes – Steak Pasty or Vegetarian Pie and they are served on paper plates! The place is usually rammed with a queue out the door every weekend. What's their secret? They make sure the pasties are the very best they could possibly offer with no gristle and plenty of filling, the pastry is light and crisp not soggy and microwaved. The pasties are sensibly priced and act as a tool to persuade people to linger for one more drink and not move off because they are hungry!

Slick service

Having a very simple menu can also minimise service issues. If the variety of food served is too broad it may lead to delays in getting the food to table due to too many cooking processes.

You only have to look at successful fast-food offerings to see how one-product offerings simplify things. KFC don't do beef, Subway don't do burgers, McDonalds don't do pizza and Pizza Hut don't do sandwiches. THIS IS FOR A REASON – not just by chance. They want to serve food fast so they need to keep all the processes really simple.

Most people are frightened of limiting choice – worried that their customers won't find anything they like. The truth is people's range of food choices is not as broad as we think it is and very often too much choice will put people off.

If you want to see this for yourself monitor the numbers that you sell of dishes on your menu. Any dish that doesn't regularly sell seven plates a day/week (depending on your scale) doesn't deserve a place on your menu.

Variations on a theme

What are you going to be?

Modern British? Italian? French? Pub Grub? Street Food? Vegetarian? There is so much choice it's important not to try and be all things to all people.

You will have a clear picture depending on your venue type, your location and your target customer, but unless the pot of cash is endless to furnish your operation with staff and equipment, it's worth considering the following when adding dishes to your menu.

1. Skill set of your chef

2. Equipment in your kitchen

3. Staff budget for food preparation

4. Component crossover in your menu

Following on from doing one thing and doing it really, really well; variations on a theme of one core dish make things much easier to manage.

Pub menus are a classic example of not sticking to this rule. You will often find a pub menu offering a range of British, Italian, Indian and Thai dishes none of which have any 'component crossover'. By this I mean each style of food has very different base ingredients: British cuisine will typically require potatoes, vegetables, meat, white fish, pastry, batter and sauces; Italian will require dough, tomatoes, salami and mozzarella; Indian will require onions, garlic and spices and Thai will require shellfish, noodles, lemongrass and herbs. It is impossible to cross over these base components and make, for example, an English menu from Thai ingredients, it just doesn't work.

When dishes on the menu are too varied, problems arise, not only with the inevitable food wastage, but service issues (waiting times from point of order to service to table) as lots of different dishes take much longer to prepare and cook, increasing wage bills for staff hours needed in preparation and service.

Component crossover

Take a leaf out of street food outlets which are rising in popularity. Influenced by worldwide travel and a broadening approach to foreign cuisines, these outlets take 'one food' and create a few variations, using the same core ingredients.

Top Tip

As I mentioned earlier: it is simply untrue that customers want massive choice. Doing one thing and doing it extremely well will generally gain you far more customers than doing 20 things averagely.

However, before you strike item after item from your menu, do consider the number of food occasions you are trying to attract your target customers to. If you are reliant on frequent visits at different times of the day, week and month, you need to consider what core dishes will be manageable but give the appearance of offering the variety each repeat visit demands. The last thing you want are your regular diners getting bored having eaten their way through your menu.

The rule of thumb is to create a variety of dishes while keeping the number of ingredients in your kitchen store to a minimum. An average pizza restaurant will have no more than 100 ingredients, as most dishes are variations on dough, mozzarella and tomato. A typical gastro pub may have maybe eight times this many ingredients.

Pizza restaurant types of main course dishes

Store cupboard ingredients - approximately 100

All dishes are made from variations on the same core ingredients

12 Pizza Varieties
4 Pasta Varieties
3 Salads
Bread and tomato at the core of every dish
Flour
Tomato Paste

Onion
Basil
Pizza meats
Toppings
Olive Oil
Salad leaves
Garlic
Pasta

Simple storage, ordering, stock management and food service as there is considerable component crossover.

Classic pub menu types of dishes

Store cupboard ingredients – approximately 800 – 1,000

Fish & chips
Pie
Sausage
Curry
Pizza
Sandwiches
Panini
Salads
Steak
Roast dinners
Lasagne and pasta
Stews
Jacket potatoes
Chicken dishes

There is a much larger range of ingredients needed to make and serve these dishes, as each will come with different accompaniments including sauces and there is very little component crossover.

 Golden Rule No.13

Big menus suck! Doing one thing and doing it well is far better than doing a hundred things unexceptionally.

Make it or buy it ready-made?

So much choice!

Your style of operation, its size, your target customer and the price points they are likely to pay will help you determine whether you should buy-in prepared products and reheat them or create everything from scratch.

Generally the higher the price points on your menu the more you can afford to go down the 'make everything from scratch' route as there will be enough margin to cover high wage costs associated with employing skilled chefs and a team of kitchen staff needed to prepare raw ingredients. There should also be enough margin to cover the inevitable food waste that comes with using fresh ingredients.

Considerations

1. **Time** - making everything from scratch takes time. If you are open for service all day you will need to factor in prep time. If you are a large-scale operation you may have this covered with a separate prep area away from service. If you are a small operation you need to consider your peak trading times and ensure there is enough downtime between busy services to make more food to sell

2. **Skill** – with a national chef shortage in the UK, you need to be sure that the 'head chef' you employed can really cut the mustard and is not some amateur who parades in head chef clothing. Be honest with yourself and work with what you've got. If you have a home-taught 'cook' as opposed to a classically-trained chef you may be better off, and more successful by letting the 'cook' focus on the service of the dishes rather than the making of the dishes

3. **Service** – generally, bought-in meals require less process in preparing them and heating them ready for customers to eat. If speedy service is your goal then prepared food will be a good option

106

4. **Consistency** – one of the key factors in getting repeat custom is to serve to the same standard time after time. If inconsistency is an issue for you, bought-in prepared products could provide the answer

5. **Waste** – fresh produce involves more waste in terms of shrinkage, shorter shelf-life and preparation. This needs to be a factor in your menu costings

6. **Storage** – daily deliveries of fresh ingredients need cold storage space. Prepared meals will require sufficient fridge/freezer space

7. **Cost** – prepared foods will generally be more expensive – this will need to be weighed against staff costs saved through not having to prepare the food

8. **Quality** – only you can determine what is the right answer here – and that is inseparably linked to the discernment of your target customers. There are some really good pre-prepared products on the market; there are also some pretty dreadful ones!

Take two highly successful and high profile London restaurants serving North African and Levantine food, of which chickpeas are a staple ingredient in many dishes. One chain buys in dried chickpeas, soaks them in vast quantities overnight then boils them until they can be used. Another buys in tinned chickpeas ready for immediate use and finds that the result is as good as using dried. They are both right. Customers love what both chains produce. But I know one of the kitchen's time, storage, stove-space - and effort are less for the same result.

9. **Portion** – pre-prepared food portions are often a bit smaller than customer expectations and can lead to disappointment. On the other hand there is no scope for staff putting too much on the plate, as the amount is pre-determined

If you're not sure what your kitchen can manage then combine a mix of fresh and bought in. Make the fresh part the star of the show and your point of difference such as special sauce or pie filling and buy in items such as pastry, bread and dessert.

Golden Rule No.14

Be realistic – the size of your kitchen and the skill of your team will determine what you buy and prepare for your customers.

Profit Vampires that put your profits in the bin, or in the staff!

In my introduction to this book, I said you would need an eye for detail to locate the many, many pots of five pence pieces that get hidden in your kitchen and reduce your profitability. I also said that you will need to introduce discipline and structure to find this extra profit that is there for the taking.

No.19 Allowing staff to help themselves

Not accounting for food consumed by staff will impact enormously on your profitability. It will also send out the wrong messages to staff. Do not encourage a 'help yourself' environment.

Profit Vampire

Staff Food

The main thing here is control – all food should be accounted for (and that includes yours, if you eat at the premises). The impact to your profitability of staff even pinching a few chips is huge. I will pause, for a second, while you shake your head with disbelief. And now, I'll give you proof that I know what I'm talking about.

Chips are, of course, eminently nibbly – but if your team help themselves as they pass through the kitchen, as much as £1,500 a year in gross profit disappears if each staff member helps themselves to a portion or so over the time of their shift.

Get a Staff Food Book and ask them to write in the details of what they have eaten every day and let them know that if you see them eating food that is not in the book they will be charged full retail price! Control your staff's consumption of your stock.

It's not just on the plate that over-portioning can occur – not using a measure to put chips into the fryer has an impact too – any leftovers usually end-up eaten by the staff - or in the bin – sometimes it can even become a 'habit' to cook a few more chips for the team to graze on.

Let me tell you about Louise, a lovely girl who worked for us: friendly, bubbly, smiley – but she could never get up in the mornings and one day she arrived a few minutes late, having dashed in missing breakfast, she asked for a piece of toast to tide her over a long shift ahead. We said, 'yes, of course'. Beware the tip of the iceberg.

Before we knew it, Louise was arriving increasingly later and later, spending the first half hour of her shift making herself now far more than humble toast – now she had progressed (unknown to us) to bacon, egg and even sausage sandwiches with, of course, a cup of tea. Not only that, she was now making the same for the five or so staff in the kitchen and bar who had looked longingly at her morning feast. So as well as providing free food for all the staff – we were also paying someone to make it! Classic!

There is always a big staff food debate – the general feeling being 'feed them or they'll take it anyway'. My personal opinion is that this is fair, but remember what I said about the detail making all the difference with food profit. Make sure there are clear guidelines as to what is and isn't acceptable or like Louise they'll be on the fillet steak before you know it! Make sure they know what time they can eat – we used to say after they'd signed-off their shift so they were not being paid to eat our food. They could eat in their own time like the rest of humanity!

In some places, where it was possible, chef would knock up a special staff meal – usually pasta-based or using up tired ingredients that would be chucked otherwise.

Profit Vampire

No.20 Not doing key line stock checks

Counting in any deliveries and monitoring any sales of a specific product to ensure nothing is going walk-ies though the day.

Rule One – everyone will steal from you. I use the word 'steal'. It's a strong, harsh word. Your staff will not think of it as stealing. You've got loads of food.

Rule Two - everyone will steal from you – even if that's just a chip or a paperclip, it's still theft.

To keep a handle on this ensure key-line stock checks are carried out every day when the kitchen closes down. Simply count high cost items such as steak, meat, fish, frozen bags of prawns – and then do the same first thing in the morning before deliveries start to arrive - it's amazing what people will take because they've run out at home! It's also a good idea to complete the key line-check by counting in any deliveries and monitoring any sales of a specific product to ensure nothing is going walkies though the day.

The key line count might look a bit like this:

1. Count a key line such as Rump steak when the kitchen opens (6.30am)
(A) 13 Rump steaks

2. Add the number of Rump steaks delivered and invoiced that day by the butcher
(B) 10 Rump steaks
A + B = 23 (C) Rump steaks

3. Sales at the end of service count the number of Rump steaks served
(C) 14 Rump steaks

4. Now count the number of Rump steaks in the meat fridge at close (11pm)
(D) 8 Rump steaks

This key line count shows you have lost one steak during the day:

(A) 13 + (B) 10 – (C) 14 = 9 there should be 9 steaks on site

Actual stock count (D) = 8

So, one steak is missing and unaccounted for and probably graced the dinner table at one of your staff's houses. Once staff see you randomly counting high cost items every night and again the next morning, then checking numbers against purchases and sales for the day, they will think twice about slipping your food in their pocket.

I didn't used to believe that my wonderful staff would steal from me until one day I had cause to call round to a manager's house unexpectedly – her mother innocently showed me in and made me a cup of coffee – in a cup and saucer exactly like we had at the pub, and funnily enough the coffee was the same brand and in the same catering size! Looking a little more closely around the kitchen waiting for the manager to come downstairs, I spotted wine bottles of a variety that were only available from our wine supplier who imported them just for us, as well as assorted 'super vitrified' crockery, again, 'just like ours'. Someone once told me it's always the member of staff that you least suspect – the ones that help you out when you're short-staffed and the ones you really think you can trust'. It couldn't have been truer!

No.21 Not allowing for yield

Beware the shrinkage associated with the cooking process – if you are basing your cost per portion on raw price per kilo, your costings could be way out.

With food items like frilly lettuce and parsley, usable quantities will inevitably reduce when the outer leaves and stalks are removed. Pickled onions may weigh 500g in the jar but a quarter of that is vinegar. With potatoes there is an obvious waste on peelings but beware the shrinkage associated with the cooking process – if you are basing your cost per portion on the raw price per kilo, your costings could be way out.

Are you getting your chips right?

It's estimated that more than 1.6 million tons of potatoes are made into chips every year in the UK (the same weight as 3,600 fully laden jumbo jets), and chips are in big demand on menus. There is even a 'National Chip Week!'

It's highly likely that your eatery will pander to the nation's love of fried potato, so if chips are on your menu, it's worth looking at their shrinkage and wastage.

As a relatively low-cost, yet bulky item, chips can enhance the perceived value of any dish – add half a portion of chips (at 20p cost) to the basic sandwich on a plate and you can increase the selling price by £1 (+75% GP) while still representing 'good value' with a hearty plateful.

There is no doubt the popularity of chips will never wane – the latest incarnation is the 'Gastro' triple-cooked chip – but with food costs increasing, particularly for prepared foods, is it really cheaper to use fresh potatoes for chips - or should you look at frozen?

Potato or prepared chips?

This is a matter of personal preference and standard of execution. I've experienced both truly greasy soggy home-made ones and some dry and flavourless frozen chips. Whatever your preference, good quality product and clean, hot oil is essential.

Undoubtedly, when done well, the crispy outside and fluffy inside of the 'triple-cooked' are unbeatable.

The big question: Are potatoes worth the hassle, and more importantly, are they as profitable as they're perceived to be?

The fact is that chips have a shrinkage element that is frequently overlooked Basing your dish costings on the raw weight of either fresh or prepared chips could impact your profitability and getting it wrong could add up to more than £5,000 a year. Here's how:

Research

Having carried out a controlled experiment using accurate scales to measure shrinkage at every stage, I can share the following facts on wastage and shrinkage of potatoes.

The experiment compared Maris Piper potatoes (90p per kilo) split into two styles of home-made chips: 'Heston Blumenthal' style triple-cooked chips and 'Classic Chip Shop' style chips.

Up against these were 'Value' frozen chips (55p per kilo) and 'Branded' frozen chips (£1.75 per kilo)

The shocking conclusion is that despite having a comparatively low price per kilo for the raw ingredient, home-made chips shrink enormously during the cooking process and can end up more expensive per portion than their convenient and prep-free counterpart – the frozen chip.

Looking at the summary of results in the comparison table shows that despite the low cost of potatoes the Triple cooked chips work out to be the most expensive and more importantly, had the dish cost been arrived at without allowing for shrinkage, it would be under-stated by 54p.

Translated into lost profit this means for every portion of triple-cooked chips sold at £3.00 and costed at 200g of raw potato allowing no shrinkage (200g @ 90p per kilo) the restaurant would believe they were achieving a very healthy 93% GP, the reality is that they would actually be making 71%. Multiply this by the number of chip portions sold annually and that discrepancy will make a big difference!

The Results

Triple-Cooked Chips	Chip Shop style	Frozen
1.25 kg Maris Piper (90p per kilo) Hand-peeled with veg knife and cut into uniform 2cm x 2cm x 6cm chips	1.25 kg Maris Piper (90p per kilo) Hand-peeled with a peeler and cut into 'chip shop' style chips	1.25 kg frozen chips 55p per kilo (value range) £1.75 per kilo (top branded)
25% weight lost in peelings	11% weight lost in peelings	0% lost in peelings
A further 30% (375g) lost in shaping chips (small potatoes discarded as they didn't make the size grade)	A further 3% (36g) lost in shaping chips (small potatoes, knobbly bits and rounded ends all made into chips)	0% lost in shaping
40% of prepped weight lost (mostly moisture) during blanching, par fry and final cooking process	41% of prepped weight lost (mostly moisture) during blanching, par fry and final cooking process	26% of prepped weight lost in cooking process
Final portion just 25% (315g) of the original raw potato weight.	Final portion 51% (639g) of the original raw potato weight	Final portion 74% (930g) of the original frozen chip weight
200g portion cost price = 72p	200g portion cost price = 35p	200g portion cost price from • 15p (value) • 43p (branded)

Golden Rule No.15

27g is 27g (not 29 or 25). Purchase a set of accurate scales and use them constantly.

The devil is in the detail

With the chips experiment, even with a potato rumbler to take care of the peeling, there is a labour cost attached to the home-made chips – the process of shaping, blanching, par frying and storing can be burdensome depending on the scale of your operation

Prepped chips are minimal cost with regards to the additional labour and have the added advantage of convenience, with easy storing for peaks and troughs in trade levels - you can hardly rustle up another 20 kilos of triple-cooked from nowhere in the middle of an unexpectedly busy service!

No.22 Not analysing the wage bill

It may be money-saving to use cheaper cuts of meat for dishes on your menu but very often these require more preparation and cooking time. If the cost-saving advantage is outweighed by the additional labour cost to prepare it (and the cost of gas/electricity to slow-cook the dish) it may not improve bottom line profits after all.

In the potato experiment, the oil used to fry the potato chips was approximately 100ml per 200g portion (and wasn't included in the costing). The frozen chips used less than half this amount as the par frying has been done for you.

Over the course of the year that could add up to 365 x 20 litre drums more for frying potatoes rather than prepared chips (based on 40 portions of chips a day).

No.23 Not allowing a cost for salt & oil

When creating your dish specifications it's important to make an allowance for oil and butter used in the cooking process, salt and pepper used to season dishes before service. Oil doesn't all get absorbed into the food it's fried in. On average 70% evaporates.

No.24 Not using specific measures

If you're not accurately measuring every portion that gets cooked you will be in danger of giving too much food on a plate - or wasting food in the cooking process.

For example, if you put just three too many chips into the fryer you may be able to re-cook once only, any more then they will spoil. Over the course of the year those three chips could add up to 165 kilos (assuming 20 portions a day) of chips that you have cooked but not served to customers.

No.25 Not getting the portion right

Giving too big a portion can be off-putting and will prevent revenue from additional sales such as desserts (generally high GP) because the diner will be too full. Getting the balance right is vital as getting your portions too small will be perceived as poor value for money.

Using dishes, boards and baskets to present your food will help ensure consistent portioning and give height to the dish making it appear 'big' without being too much. Invest in attractive wire presentation baskets resembling mini fryer baskets that come in many shapes and sizes as these not only look more impressive than a pile of chips on a plate but also help keep a handle on portion control.

Over-portioning by just two chips (12.5g each) could cost you dearly. At 40 portions of chips a day, just two chips too many on every portion comes to 365 kg of chips a year with a cost of £1,315 (Heston); £638 (chip shop) or £240-£730 (frozen)

Selling them at 70% GP instead of giving them away prevents a loss of up to £3k from your bottom line. So getting the portion just right is crucial – to both customer satisfaction and your profit margin.

Pros and cons of potato vs prepared chips:

The Humble Spud	Prepared Chips
Raw ingredient price increases are passed on immediately – can squeeze your margins	Can secure a fixed price or negotiate prices held
You choose how to cut to size – giving options to make a chip 'statement' with chunky chips	Long life and convenience
	Less waste than fresh
You can leave skin on and customize	Less labour cost than fresh
Flavour - Maris Piper are generally believed to be the best – but check out Yukon Gold and Highland Burgundy Reds heritage varieties as well	Higher energy cost – if chips are cooked from frozen the temperature of the oil will drop and use more power to get back up to full heat
Uses more oil in the cooking process	Variety – they come in a wide range of quality, styles and sizes
Higher labour cost and waste considerations	Storage – drop a box of frozen skinny fries when they are frozen and the shattered sticks will only produce half the normal portions
Excellent flavour and crispness give great customer satisfaction	Ease – sometimes life's too short to peel a spud

In case you're wondering... what are triple-cooked chips?

- Uniform in size – like Jenga pieces

- Part-cooked in boiling salted water (Heston cooks his until they are nearly falling apart – but this makes handling them tricky). Drained and chilled

- Fried at 130 degrees for approximately 5 minutes

- Drained and chilled again (popping in the freezer draws out more moisture)

- Par-fried they can be kept chilled for up to three days

- Finished by frying at 180 degrees for approximately 7 minutes. This makes the coating crispy and the inside lovely and fluffy

Beware the Sunday Vampires

Sunday lunch is a big eating-out occasion

In fact it's the biggest regular event in the pub industry – accounting for 22% of pub food sales weekly. The pub roast dinner is worth £876 million (CGA Strategy report Nov 2012) and represents 68% of all meals sold in pubs on a Sunday.

With so much at stake it is surprising to find operators are not making the profit they should from this big day. The principles here aren't exclusive to roasts, they can apply to pretty much any 'big day' food event.

No.26 Not planning your Sunday roasts

Do you intend to run out? This can create demand as well as disappoint – but will guarantee NO WASTE. Will you guess and throw away what's left (particularly veg, spuds and Yorkies)?

Will you 'best guess' and run out sometimes but use the leftovers in 'specials' or normal menu lines?

Shrinkage

The 'yield' or amount of meat you have to sell after it has been cooked can vary enormously depending on how long it has been cooked. Moist heat in the cooking process will reduce the shrinkage. If you don't have a Rationale Combi oven (if only!) ensure meat is well covered during cooking, and is cooked for the minimum amount of time necessary.

- Some chefs stand joints in water during oven cooking
- Cut large joints into 2 – 3 to reduce cooking time
- Try a long, slow cook overnight at 100 degrees C

No.28 Not carving meat accurately

Carving meat straight from the oven is a talent and demands skill – the meat needs to be well-rested and each slice needs to be the correct thickness and presented beautifully on the plate. By cutting the meat too thickly you will reduce, or wipe out, your profit.

If you're not sure you have the skill to carve straight from the oven, carve cold and rewarm: when cold a joint is much firmer and will enable you to be accurate with your carving. It also makes service much quicker. Randomly weigh portions every service to check accuracy.

No.29 Not updating prices

Food costs fluctuate constantly and if a key ingredient rises significantly without a corresponding retail price change it will erode your margins – particularly if it's a staple such as potato or butter.

Wherever possible negotiate fixed term prices on significant ingredients and change your menu to correspond with the time period you have fixed for. Use a specials board for seasonal things so you can take them off when prices change. Use descriptions like 'Veg of the day' and 'Fish of the day' to give you flexibility to vary these to the best market price

No.30 Not monitoring meat price

Meat prices fluctuate more than most food items, and even if you have an accurate and fully-costed dish specification you will need to keep a close eye to check margins are not being eroded. Pricing varies according to the cut and whether it has the bone in or out. You need to take this into account and choose your meat according to the price point you have decided on for your roasts.

No.31 Not planning your potatoes

Count how many potatoes constitute a portion and stick to it. If your portion is generous (roast spuds are a great feel good value add), make sure you cost this in to the dish spec rather than end up giving 'extras' for free

Potatoes can increase in price significantly (a 7.5% rise in a just a few months in 2013) and are too expensive to be wasteful with.

Increase yield - if you peel them yourself check the peelings are 'see-through' thin.

Decide, as near as you can, to the optimal size of roastie you will serve and make sure all roasties are cut to that specification.

If you cook and serve roasties on the day, stagger times they go in the oven to match the peaks and troughs in service.

Par-cook your roasties in advance and 'flash' them in the fryer to crisp and heat through.

No.32 Not buying seasonally

Veg can be expensive out of season and can add £'s to your wage bill in prep time. Broccoli and cauliflower don't 'hold' very well during service. Carrots are a good staple as is cabbage, choose other veg according to season, your price point and margin.

We are now used to being able to buy any product we like – particularly fruit and veg – throughout the year because our supply chains now facilitate this. There are, however, best times to buy certain products when they are plentiful, fresh and cheaper. Always check with suppliers as to what's in season each week before you plan your accompaniments and dishes.

Monitor your portions during a whole service through checking the veg that comes back into the kitchen uneaten by scraping it all into a tub. If the tub is full adjust your portions.

Consider putting veg on the plate rather than in bowls if your volumes allow (it's hard to get veg on the plate fast enough in busy pubs). As an 'added value', offer your customers free extra veg on demand but make sure you have costed this in. The chances are 50% will decline but will appreciate the option. A mix of frozen and fresh may be cost-effective and appropriate for your customer base.

No.33 Cold food that should be hot

Food not arriving at the customer's table at the right temperature
Everyone wants to avoid customer complaints (as these usually result in food wastage) so it's essential to set-up a slick system that means food isn't left waiting around before waiting staff take it to table. It needs to arrive piping hot and beautifully presented.

This means getting staffing levels right for peak times and having heat lamps on the pass to keep things warm while they are being dished up.

It can be a challenge 'assembling' roast dinners to ensure the meals are served together and piping hot. It is a huge waste of resources and profit to be reheating roasts or throwing food away due to customer complaints.

- Plates need to be piping hot
- Piping hot gravy will lift the temperature of the meal
- Flash roasties in the fryer or microwave if necessary and if veg is microwaved and served separately, ensure it is heated through and not standing too long before it's served.

No.34 Not costing condiments

When creating your dish specifications it's important to make an allowance for condiments such as mustard, tomato sauce, mayonnaise, horseradish etc.

If you serve your condiments, ramekin size is vital – too big and you will be throwing away a lot of unrequired sauce – one operator I know washes up the miniature preserve glass jars and lid and fills these with condiments – they are a perfect size and imaginative method of presentation.

Sunday is a big condiment day with mint sauce, horseradish, English mustard and apple sauce as standard. Ensure these are accounted for in your dish costings.

No.35 Not factoring extra staff costs

For many, the addition of a Sunday roast is like running a separate business on this one day of the week. Some pubs run entirely different menus Mon- Saturday so there is little or no crossover of component in-gredients, making the prep list on a Sunday much longer. This can soon mount-up to lots of extra people-hours to carry out all the different processes, for example, gravy, veg peeling and preparation, Yorkshire puds and roast meats, few of which you would normally serve during the rest of the week.

No.36 Running too big a menu

Running too big a menu, particularly on a Sunday, can lead to service issues. Keep the menu simple by removing a lot of the time-consuming and fiddly items you run the rest of the week. Too much choice will lead to service glitches.
Remember 64% of pub meals sold on a Sunday are roast dinners. You will not put your customers off by running a smaller menu.

Golden Rule No.16

Planning is everything – put in place a system to ensure you order and prepare the correct volumes of food.'

5 The other stuff – the stuff no-one tells you!

Don't be...

...the best kept secret in town!

One of the biggest failings of every independent restaurant, every independent pub and every independent food operator in the UK is they fail to grasp the importance of marketing their business. Clinging on to the hope that still in the 21st century 'word of mouth' and an ad in the local rag will be enough to sustain and grow a profitable business.

Who knows you're there?

Back in the 90's we had a pub two miles up a country lane from a very busy tourist attraction that had over 100,000 visitors a year. In the school summer holidays we got a bit of trade but not nearly as much as the two big managed houses that visitors passed on their way into the zoo. Frustrated because no-one that visited the zoo knew we existed, we chatted up the local nursery operator who owned the land opposite the exit to the zoo car park and persuaded him (a few free meals and pints) to let us put a sign in the tree prominent at the exit with a big arrow pointing left – instead of right past the pubs on the way in. We backed this up with some A1-laminated posters at the exit – showing happy children playing in our beautiful country garden. The result - we attracted another £35k of trade during the six weeks of the summer!

There are three ways to grow your business:

1. Get new customers

2. Get existing customers to buy from you more frequently

3. Get customers to spend more each visit

In order to do any of these you need to make a lot of noise.

Getting new customers is hard – what makes you think they notice your ad?

In an average day your potential customer is likely to see over 3,000 separate advertising messages - and buried deep down under a mountain of other 'great deals' and 'best services' is your message and it is asking a lot of even the most studious of customers to give it some of their head space.

Add to this their boredom with seeing so many marketing messages and their immunity to most calls to action and we have a problem. However - the good news is that people will ALWAYS like to be amused, entertained and even shocked and that gives those that are willing to try a great opportunity. It stands to reason that the more outrageous your advertising, the more chance you have of getting your business noticed. Add to this a killer product, offer or service and you're on to a winner.

BUT of course it is never that simple:

- How much money have you got to let them know you exist?
- How do you know the money you spend on marketing is really working?
- How do you stand out from the crowd?

There are 45 marketing methods your business can use (see Chapter 7 for the full list). In the next few pages I discuss the main ones to consider.

Golden Rule No.17

Everyone advertises they do 'great food.' Don't be beige with your marketing – dare to be different and stand out from the crowd or your marketing efforts will be a complete waste of time and money.

Marketing

Here are some of the main methods to consider:

1. **Ad in the paper** – isn't that what everyone else does? It lacks imagination, is costly but if you do it make sure you have a way of measuring its effectiveness – use a redemption offer such as 'bring this voucher to receive half price/ 25% off/free glass of fizz' (add to this redemption an email address and phone number and you can increase your database too!)
    At the very least use a call tracking number – so you can see how many people have phoned in response to that particular ad. You may think your ad is the best designed 'stand out' from the crowd – but when nestled amongst 20 other restaurants all offering a special menu, the reader may not see the same

2. **Editorial in the paper** – journalists are always looking for a story. This is free publicity – just keep your imagination open for a story with local appeal. Readers will be more interested in a 'true story' than an ad

3. **A-boards** – great if well done. Not too many words and an eye-catching message will have the most impact. 'Great Food, Great Beer, Great Atmosphere' is probably the most overused pub A-board sign that really blends into the background

Take a tip from Pete at The Mailman, Yeovil – his A board reads: 'Cold food, warm beer, grumpy landlord – don't believe us come in and see.' By cleverly instilling some humour into those few words and tackling customer experience in other venues where they may indeed have been sold cold foot that should be hot, served lukewarm beer that should be chilled and served by a rude or disinterested person behind the bar, Pete has crafted a really powerful marketing message that stands out from the crowd!

4. **Make headlines** - any piece of marketing you write – whether it's a flyer, a poster, an ad or even an email will be a complete waste of time and money if it doesn't get read. Always spend time crafting a headline that will get you noticed. Use power words like 'How to...'; New'; 'Free'; 'Discover'; 'Guaranteed'; 'Fast' and 'You'. A good headline will identify the reader and make them want to find out more. 'They lived happily ever after' – the reader wants to continue to find out how!

'Men! How to get more brownie points this Valentine's Day,' is a far better headline to advertising your Valentine's menu than: 'Book now for Valentine's Day,' as it draws the reader (probably men) into the copy as they want to find out more – men could always use a few more brownie points! Similarly: 'Three reasons to book for lunch at the Red Restaurant,' will intrigue the reader far more than a standard 'Red Restaurant Lunch Menu'

5. **Offers** – use special offers to 'hook' new customers. An offer needs to be sufficiently attractive to get the person to take action. A blanket 10% off is unimaginative, not compelling enough to trigger action and will probably just reduce your profit without increasing trade (you may well end up simply rewarding customers who would have been with you anyway and paying full price). Offers should have a deadline and as already mentioned, a 'redemption' part that means you can measure the number of people that have responded to the offer (and justify the spend) and collect data from those attending to add to your database

6. **Social Media** – It's free – but it can be a big time waster – make sure you have a clearly defined purpose for your social media – engagement with your loyal customers – direct marketing of offers and events and general news of menus and food. Instagram pictures of your food and make your customers salivate

7. **Testimonial sites** – no-one sells your business better than happy customers – and yet everyone focuses on the negativity around sites such as TripAdvisor.

Two things: even if you refuse to go on Twitter or facebook – it's where your customers are and where your competitors are. Handled well it will give you a voice and help you keep your ear to the ground if customers complain about niggly things, it could be worth a listen before you dismiss it – it is almost like having your very own mystery shopper. If they say the table was in a draught – sit at it and experience what they did – they could be right. Drown out negative comments by making it part of your routine to ask for testimonials from happy customers – no-one believes all those shiny sites with nothing but glowing reports anyway – a few grumbles makes you human and a well thought out response can turn a complaining customer into a top customer – see the real life case study in Chapter 2

8. **Website** – first impressions count – is there is scope to make yours better? Keep content fresh, changing and relevant and Google will love you. Lots of top quality pictures of food and surroundings will say more than a thousand words of text

9. **Newsletters** – e-news or hard copy are a fantastic way of promoting special events and creating a customer community. Avoid the temptation to 'sell,' instead 'add value' and entertain in your newsletter to create loyalty and interest

10. **Database** – this really is the secret weapon of any food operator. If you can find ways to collect contact details (comment cards, competitions, facebook gateways, special offer coupons, loyalty cards, booking details) you have the opportunity to talk to your customers again when you have another occasion, special offer or event.
This is known as direct marketing and is highly effective as you can segment your database for different types of customer and communicate with each segment only about stuff that you know will appeal to them

11. **Having a 'loyalty' scheme** - at the heart of your data capture makes sense as it not only gives a valid reason for people to give you their contact info and a way for you to build your database, but also presents an opportunity to 'wow' your customers if you collect the right data. I have used companies such as Explosive Marketing to manage this for me. When people sign up for their free VIP membership card they are asked for their birthday, their partner's birthday, their anniversary and that sort of thing. They then use these occasions to communicate with them (birthday cards) to nudge them back into the restaurant. They also use other events such as Mothers' Day and Valentine's to do the same. They even have a 'Your birthday just wasn't the same without you,' card which gets sent a couple of weeks after their birthday if they didn't pay a visit. This one gets a great response – 20% respond, and people love the fact you noticed!

12. **PR** – all PR (short for Public Relations) means is giving something – whether it's time, product, or money, or sponsorship, in return for 'exposure.' This can be one of the most effective ROI's – particularly with the advent of social media which allows your story to get in front of the journalists who are always using it to trawl for a story. Good PR has the potential to go viral very quickly – often culminating in national press, TV and radio exposure.

At our Cornish pub/restaurant we made great returns on PR (Chef Chris Adey's idea). Without being asked we daily sent a couple of branded cold boxes down to the lifeguards who patrolled the beach May – Sept. These were filled with cold soft drinks and ice to refresh them during the day. The exposure we got for our philanthropy? They became our best advocates – always recommending our place to visitors and often signing off for the day on the Tannoy announcing they were going to the place that does the 'Best Food in Cornwall.'

Or what about a quick thinking publican, Mickey Thomson, he hit the headlines and ended up with a quarter page spread in the Sunday Times completely FOC by pouncing on a sentence most people would ignore, and through FB and Twitter making a viral story and gaining great PR for his pub. What did he do? All he did was pick up on a throwaway line the MP Eric Pickles said when he was being interviewed by Kirsty Young on Radio 4's Desert Island Discs. Pickles said as an aside 'I'm a Yorkshire man but my heart is in

Essex,' that's all – but quick thinking Mickey (a Yorkshire man himself running a pub in Yorkshire) immediately broadcast on Social Media that Eric Pickles was banned from his pub as he was a 'traitor to the north' – it very soon went viral with the press and TV getting hold of it and giving great exposure to Mickey and his pub!

13. **Food events** – from farmers markets to chilli festivals, to themed nights or oyster festivals, introducing a food 'special' event will keep the interest of your customers and staff alike. If you find yourself wishing it could be Christmas every day, food events can be the next best thing, but be warned they are hard work to organize, can disrupt normal service and require the skills set of the kitchen team to be appropriate for the event's nature. However, if you want to increase frequency of visit and bring in new custom then these are a good thing to do

Top Tip

Most people like to try new experiences but hate change! A food event will give them a chance to try something new in a familiar and safe environment. If someone has always wanted to try Thai food but doesn't want to make an idiot of themselves ordering the wrong stuff in a proper Thai restaurant (and potentially wasting money on food they don't like) – going to a Thai taster themed night at their local restaurant where they are known and where an element of 'learning' is added into the process is much more appealing.

14. **Guest chef** – a novel experience for all would be Masterchefs – invite a guest chef to cook a one night slot in the kitchen; if you don't happen to have a tame celebrity chef why not give a customer a chance – it would be big prestige to win a chance to cook in the kitchen. Make sure you give a consideration for EHO food safety though.

I once had the opportunity to help prepare a starter in Ramsay at Claridges (Chef's Table where we saw all the workings!) It was really exciting – and also really reassuring to see that the processes and methods we employed in our own pub-restaurant kitchen were exactly the same as the great man's – the main difference was one of scale ... and quality of equipment!

Marketing spend

You will only know if the money you spend on marketing is working if you continuously measure it. Redemptions, bounce back offers (visit us next January and 2 dine for half price – date and quiet period specific). Call tracking numbers – having a specific phone number (these are readily available from call management companies and most will give you local codes, your phone line is set exactly as now but you purchase additional phone numbers – they simply sit on top of your existing phone line and your staff answer the phone in exactly the same way) for every piece of marketing – particularly that ad in the paper. Ask them to ring you as the call to action and the measure the number of responses.

Creating loyal customers will reap rewards: satisfaction should be your foundation, loyalty your aspiration. Once you understand the lifetime value of a loyal customer (see Chapter 2) you can afford to invest in finding more customers just like them through effective marketing.

Golden Rule No.18

Only lazy or incompetent restaurant owners don't create a database and measure the success of their marketing.

Try not to poison your customers

Food safety basics

Knowing the five common food poisoning bacteria gave me confidence in handling the inevitable customer complaint regarding alleged food poisoning. I first discovered the power of the words, 'visit the doctor with a stool sample,' in early 2000 and ever since found this ghastly sentence essential to handling such a delicate predicament.

The fact is that, rightly or wrongly, a customer will usually blame the last meal they ate before they get ill. The phone call the next day – 'I ate with you last night; I've been up all night being violently sick and with terrible diarrhoea.'

Unless it's Staphylococcus (which tends not to involve diarrhoea), the onset period for symptoms is usually more than 12 hours, but your customer will be in a distressed state making it really difficult to tactfully say: 'It's probably not us but something you had for breakfast yesterday.'

How to deal with it?

Give the customer lots of sympathy: something along the lines of 'I'm so sorry you're feeling ill, that's really terrible. We take this matter very seriously and would like to establish some facts so we may investigate and record your complaint.'

Then ask:

- What time did you eat with us?
- What did you drink?
- What menu items did you eat with us?
- What else did you have to eat during the day and where?

Once you've established the facts you introduce the clincher: 'Have you been to the doctor?' If the answer is 'no' you need to say 'What we need you to do is go to the doctors with a stool sample to identify the bacteria.'

This really sorts the men from the boys and sends those who are trying it on heading for the hills.

It also gives you a chance to take control of the situation and take the necessary action (freeze a sample of the dish if possible, check your prep, storage, cooking and probe records, all of which will all help your defence and demonstrate due diligence).

The science of compliance

If you are involved in the preparation and service of food, you and your team will need to comply with all the rules and regulations regarding food safety. I'm not going into too much detail here, there are plenty of courses and books out there to do that.

Key things you need to know:

Poor food hygiene is bad for business – it takes years to gain a reputation, it takes days to gain a bad one.

Don't count yourself above this - this is not the reserve of the greasy spoons, the freshest ingredients don't mean much if they've got Salmonella and most chefs don't have Salmonella X-ray specs. Remember, one of the UK's most high profile restaurants, The Fat Duck owned by Heston Blumenthal, was closed after customers complained of food poisoning. It made the national news. It was not good news for Heston's business and profits.

Other examples include Leicester City Council health inspectors who fell ill following a night out at a popular Indian restaurant due to Salmonella. The restaurant had only ever had five star health and safety ratings in the past, but had to close immediately.

Or Quaglinos, one of London's leading restaurants, whose clients included Sir Mick Jagger and Sir Elton John, took a long time to recover from the highly publicised Oystergate. One poor customer, celebrating her 50th birthday, Denise Martin, died after eating oysters from the restaurant's 'oyster altar' in 2009. This is a personal thing, but it is fair comment for me to say that I, Ali Carter, would never eat at such a restaurant again.

To minimise risk follow these six simple rules:

1. **Qualifications** - check chef has up-to-date certificates (Food Safety Level 2 minimum and Level 3 for your key staff)

2. **Label** - use a date-dot system to record when dishes were made and fresh ingredients bought

3. **Hygiene** - use Sanitizer and blue roll paper in preference to cloths. (Ensure the Sanitizer is made-up to the correct ratio and less than 4 hours old)

4. **Cooking temperature** - have a food temperature probe and routinely record and probe dishes

5. **Chill** - record fridge and freezer temperatures daily

6. **Cross contamination** - ensure all staff understand about cross-contamination

'Scores on the Doors.'

You will be marked by your Environmental Health Officer following an inspection, between 1-5 out of 5 for cleanliness and food safety. Five out of five is the top mark. However much you may hate the seemingly endless red tape involved in recording and monitoring storage, food temperatures and preparation methods for the EHO, it is worth it for peace of mind. You really don't want to poison your customers. Also, proving you run a safe business, and getting those lovely 5 stars to display, is a valuable benchmark against the competition. It is already compulsory to display these marks out of five in food premises in Wales - letting your customers know your score is a useful marketing tool.

Ask yourself why would anyone risk visiting you for less than 4 stars? Even if you're a kebab shop you'll be up against other fast food offerings that will have 5 stars. A score of 5 really should be your base line – who wants to eat in a place that proclaims via the star system that it is only averagely clean?

1. **Salmonella** – found in raw milk, raw eggs, raw poultry. Typical symptoms include abdominal pain, diarrhoea, vomiting and fever (lasts 1-7 days) Onset period is usually 12-36 hours

2. **Bacillus cereus** – found in cereals, especially rice, dust and soil. Typical symptoms include vomiting, abdominal pain and some diarrhoea lasting 1 – 2 days. Onset period is usually 1-6 hours

3. **Clostridium botulinum** - found in soil, fish, meat and vegetables. Typical symptoms include difficulties in swallowing, talking and breathing, double vision and paralysis of the cranial nerves. Fatalities are common and the recovery of survivors may take several months. Onset period usually 12-36 hours

4. **Staphylococcus aureus** – found in human nose, mouth, skin, boils and cuts; raw milk from cows or goats. Typical symptoms include abdominal pain, mainly vomiting, some diarrhoea, low temperature (lasts 6-24 hours). Onset period can be 1-7 hours – usually 2-4

5. **Clostridium perfringens** – found in animal and human excreta, soil (on vegetables) dust, insects and raw meat. Typical symptoms include abdominal pain and diarrhoea – vomiting is rare, lasts 12-48 hours. Onset of symptoms 8-12 hours

Golden Rule No.19

Cleanliness brings peace of mind. Although no one likes the paperwork, insist your team complies with the rules for food safety.

Open your eyes to what your customers see

First impressions and all that

Without you realising it your customers are constantly taking in non-food clues as to what to expect at your place and that starts even before they step foot through the door.

In fact it can often start before they even arrive in your road – your online image will determine in many cases if people will even get close – more about that in Chapter 5.

Run-a-restaurant books are filled with 'check lists' advising restaurateurs and publicans on how to (and I hate this cliché) 'walk the customer journey.' They advise you to look with fresh eyes at the exterior of your premises and check – no peeling paint, free of litter and cigarette butts, well-lit, well-signposted, well-hazard-analysed, plants alive and well-tended, no weeds, no dirty windows. It's pretty much standard stuff and comes down to having standards and values that are in line with your style of outlet.

Once you understand that everything is a deliberate and positive creation you can really get the detail right – and this is what counts in the context of your menu

1. **Menus** – Chapter 3 looks in detail at this vital bit of kit - style, fonts and layouts. But the quality of your menu - weight of paper and professionalism of layout and print will count – as will the stickiness, glass ring stains and dog-earedness.

2. **Marketing materials** – other stuff you have around the place from wall posters (there's only so much clip art one can bear – particularly if the food offer is top end) to table-talkers. I once sat down to a posh Christmas lunch where my

place was reserved with a sign that was so ancient it looked like it had been through the washing machine. The point was there's nothing I could complain about – my place was reserved – there was nothing wrong. But there was nothing right about it either – and the truth is it made me feel unloved. And while we're on the subject of reserved signs, it annoys me when I reserve a table and when my guests and I turn up, I see 'Carter,' on a piece of paper. My name isn't Carter. It is Alison Carter, or Ms Carter. Just putting the surname is plain rude. How hard is it to put a Mr or Mrs or Ms or, heaven forbid, find out the first name of the person who's about to put £100 into your till?

3. Crockery, glassware, cutlery and napkins - all frame your food and add to its perceived value. As a general rule of thumb – posh food needs very superior plates, knives and forks, glassware and napkins.

Basic food needs basic plates – so generally the lower the price points on your menu the more you can scrimp on the crocks. But do give a lot of consideration to the platform your food arrives at the table on – a humble burger and chips can be transformed in customer perceived value by presenting it on a larger plate or on a chopping board. There was a trend at one time for serving certain dishes on a slate – these dishes looked fabulous in terms of presentation but were actually rather tricky to eat as there were no 'edges' to help diners scoop food onto the fork.

Putting basic food on a posher plate might mean you can charge a bit more – but it doesn't work the other way round!

Chipped or cracked crockery is a no-no whoever you are. As are hot meals served on cold plates. Do not do this.

Big plates are great for presenting impressive looking dishes but how many can a waitress carry at once? If you're a high speed food operation you will need to consider this.

Château Lafite will definitely not taste as good to your customer if drank out of a line-marked Paris goblet rather than a crystal wide-bowled glass. Getting your glassware right is vital to matching customer expectations, but has to be balanced with the practicalities of cost, thin stemmed crystal glasses may be perfect – but not necessarily the right choice if half a dozen break every time a tray is put through the glass washer or as staff polish them.

The quality, style and weight of your cutlery is important too – this needs to reflect the style of food and be appropriate for every course and dish.

Ditto napkins – even if you're a mid to low-end operation don't dismiss linen napkins in favour of paper – or the heavier 'Benders' napkins. If your diners are likely to get through three or more paper ones (one per course) then linen may well be a cost-effective way as linen stays with you through the meal rather than being scrunched up and discarded as each course is taken away.

Top Tip

Always cost your napkin price, or linen laundering price, into a dish cost as it is a vital component of every plate of food.

4. **Condiments**– test every salt and pepper pot daily to make sure they are 'flowing' but also invest in them with a not 'the-cheapest-because-everyone-pinches-them' mentality. If your food style would be better matched with 'finer' versions of your current salt and pepper pots then it's up to you to train the staff to 'manage' their use i.e. removing them after the main course when clearing the table to avoid customers 'accidently' slipping them into their handbag.

5. **Bric-a-brac and pictures on the wall** – remember YOU are not your customer – what you personally like has no place here. Remember two things:

Think theatrical – not domestic – this means size, scale and impact. You can get away with giant mirrors, furniture and pictures to enhance your food stage.

Bric-a-brac and pictures - set the mood and feel of the place and deserve much thought.

A top-end pub restaurant I visited recently spoiled the ambience completely by displaying a local artist's pictures that were at odds with the overall look and feel of the place both in colours and style. Matters were made even worse by the Day-Glo price stars attached to each one. Either be a restaurant or a gallery – or at the very least if you have a local artist who wants to fill your walls with their stuff make sure it's professional looking – not amateur and ill-suited to your whole food offer.

6. **Service area/bar** – this focal point whether it's a bar, a counter or a waiting station can be a great display space to promote products and events rather than a dumping ground for all the practical clobber needed to serve. Look and really see what your customers see. You're not selling old half-pint glasses stuffed with ball-point pens and keys, an 'adorable' cuddly toy given by a customer or cheap darts trophies.

7. **Blackboards** – if you use chalkboards please remember that Day-Glo chalk pens are only appropriate in Working Men's Clubs and dives. I'm sure there are those that disagree and say it's a matter of taste – but seriously – who's taste? If it's yours I refer you to the 'You are not your customer' statement above.

It seems blindingly obvious but you need clear writing that doesn't dip off the end of the board, correct spelling and a simple clear message in writing big enough to be read from a distance. The board is for your customers not for you so look at it from their perspective. Avoid clichés and try and have some fun on the boards and they'll be more effective.

8. **Loos** – never underestimate the power and influence of the loo over the decision to visit your establishment. Women in particular will make a subconscious decision whether to revisit based on the quality and cleanliness of your loos alone! In fact 29% of people just wouldn't come back according to a recent Harris Interactive poll. Let's face it if

your loos are a bit tatty, or worse still, grubby, your customers (88% according to Harris) will judge that the rest of your business is the same – which implies your kitchen – where their food is prepared. Do you blame them – if what they can see is less than pristine, what's it like where they can't see – your kitchens and store rooms?

The quality of loo rolls, hand-creams, hand-driers or paper towels needs to match (or exceed) the quality of your food offer and the prices you are charging.

9. **Temperature** – 'climate control' is the silent customer judge of your premises – people will only notice when you get it wrong. There are some simple things you can do – such as if you have an open fire make sure it's lit at least an hour before you open the doors so the first customers through the door are greeted with glowing warmth and not a smoking squib. The general rule is that the higher the price points on your menu the more attention you should pay to achieving the perfect ambient temperature at all times – that means air conditioning and decent heating.

Oh, one thing: if customers keep their coats on while with you, they're telling you that your place is colder than their house - and it is unlikely they'll return. Temperature of plates? Hot food on hot plates and cold food not on hot plates – do I really need to say that again?

10. **Chairs** - a lot more thought than anticipated should go into matching your chairs to your menu. Most operators tend to go for the cheaper end of the market simply because they are under-capitalised for furniture spend. This is a mistake. Consider your food, your style of operation and your menu price points – do you want customers to linger over a leisurely three courses and stay chatting into the night at the table buying high GP desserts, digestifs and coffees? If so you will need to provide chairs that won't numb the parts that matter. If the seat is too hard people will fidget after an hour or so and may not decide to return again – probably never really knowing themselves why. If you want to turn your tables or if your average meal sold is a snack or simple one

course, then chairs at the comfiest end of the scale would be a mistake as guests will linger – making it harder to turn the tables.

Music – mood killer or mood creator? Remember you are not your customer so personal taste (or the taste of your staff) should not come into it. To reflect your customer base you will need to consider different categories of music at different times of the day and the week. You can vary the tempo and volume of the music according to how empty you are and the sort of 'vibe' or atmosphere you want to create.

The right choice of music for your diners will make them feel they 'belong'. Science shows that music we listened to in our formative teenage years has strong emotional power to help us form bonds with a place where we hear it – use the power of nostalgia to create that loyal bond by playing music from the teenage years of your customer base. For example, if your customers are in their thirties play music from the nineties. If your customer base are in 50's and 60's play music from 1960's and 1970's.

You can also use music to help turn tables (speed up the tempo) or sell more courses (slow the tempo down).

Juke box – if you think this may be appropriate for your outlet, you will be putting the atmosphere created in your place totally in the hands of your customers. Great when things are going well – particularly giving customers a chance to hook into the nostalgia aspect of re-hearing songs from their past. But bear in mind the mood of a place can change in a second depending on the music played – going from the Beatles to AC/DC could really upset some of your customers. Best to stick to one genre of music appropriate to your core customer base.

Put markers on the volume control – for different times of day. Create playlists with different styles of music for different times of the day e.g. easy listening for middle-aged lunch time trade, up-tempo between 5-7pm for creating atmosphere as guests arrive. Wallpaper/bland music is a lazy option and has a negative impact. It says to your customers subliminally 'we can't be bothered to think about the music you might enjoy' and it can have a negative impact on repeat custom.

In one of our pubs my husband would put on a crazy selection of music at closing time – to encourage people to leave – songs like Jerusalem, Tie Me Kangaroo Down and Stairway to Heaven – the late night eclectic music became legendary quite quickly and the hope that it would clear the place backfired as people would actually hang on to the bitter end to have a sing along!

Golden Rule No.20

The dining experience goes way beyond the food.
Pay attention to the detail of the environment you create
for your guests.

The hidden detail

Otherwise known as 'the context of the sale' (does your gaff look right) and more importantly, does it match customers' expectations?

The simple truth is that the food experience extends way beyond the food itself.

Alan Yau, founder of the massively successful restaurant chain Wagamamas, understood this. He realised that the Wagamama concept would be based on the simplicity of a single product with three components – soup, noodles and toppings. But his level of detail reached way beyond the food.

He described the lines of communal tables at 90 degrees to an open kitchen as a perfect 'dynamic' relationship that could be applied to any type of cuisine.

Yau talks about forming the 'emotional architecture' of a restaurant. He believes that there are perfect dimensions for table size and height to create the optimal dining experience based on the dimensions used by Harry's Bar in Venice. Tables should be 680mm in height and 600mm in depth, with seat height at a fixed and unchanging 380mm. Table lighting should be Osram Halospot with the power at 50 watts and the angle of the lamp at eight degrees. He loves ceiling fans creating a flow of air around a restaurant.

He says the space given to each customer should be around one metre square. 'The tighter the circulation space, the more you are able to build the intimacy of that space. The energy you are able to create from this is incredible.' Yau also applies Feng Shui to each restaurant twice over – a first fix of Feng Shui followed by a second. 'I'm seeking harmony through the arrangement of space,' he said. Yau was ordained as a Buddist monk in 2010 and he told his audience that at each new venue 'he meditates in the space where we want to develop a concept'. At the end of Yau's cerebral presentation he had one last ethereal observation: 'concept development should be more than the articulation of space.'

Source - Paul Charity, Propel Conference

Now, it would tempting to dismiss the above as inappropriate to your business, and all a bit airy-fairy, but I take it seriously for two reasons. Alan Yau has created something original and different to the dining out experience, and he is very, very successful. We can learn from him.

While 'meditating the space' may seem a step too far for many, it's important to be in charge of the environment your guests will eat in

In all our restaurants we used to sit at every table, try every chair regularly. This came about because our staff started referring to one of the tables as the 'toilet table' Having sat at this table and experienced the steady flow of customers on their way to the loo and the draft caused by the swing of the doors (and the occasional waft of odour) as they came and went, we knew we had to build a shielding partition and put better ventilation in the loos, turning 'toilet table' into a much more comfortable and secluded place to eat!

Things to consider:

- Chairs that are too low for a table – even by just a couple of centimetres - can be the unseen factor in dwindling trade.

- Tables in the middle of the room are viewed as second class – unless the place is rammed, as guests feel vulnerable and exposed.

- Padded booths are lovely – but how easy is it for guests to get in and out?

- How you divide up the space matters. Window tables, and tables set in niches will always be popular as an air of intimacy is created. The communal canteen style of Yau is unique – but doesn't happen by accident.

- It's all about what you think it should look like when perfect, it's what you stand for. Customers will move things, staff will move things and it's your job to keep moving things back to how you want it. One very successful operator I recently met said his job was basically to go around picking the cigarette butts out of the flowerpots. He was joking but it's a very valid point.

- Once you think of yourself, as the 'creator' of your premises who takes positive actions in every aspect of the physical environment, you will be one step closer to getting the detail right.

'I want to be alone'

George and Sonia syndrome

Nothing can prepare you for being an employer. I feel so strongly about this, that I'll say it again, but in a different way. Employing people is a job in itself.

I vowed after we sold our last licensed restaurant and hotel business never to employ again. Having created 50 full and part- time jobs in a part of the country where unemployment was high, I felt it was a thankless task and guaranteed to disappoint. I have since got over that bitter pill realising that to try and do everything myself is a sure fire ticket to the funny farm, early grave and bankruptcy.

I had a bad experience with two employees: Let's call them 'George' and 'Sonia' – who knew more than me about their rights as employees and were determined to create a scenario at tribunal to fleece us for alleged, and completely unfounded, discrimination on every level. It was particularly galling and frustrating as 'George' and 'Sonia's' work fell below the standards that I insisted upon - but that didn't seem to matter when it came to employment law!

Staff is one of the few areas where as a business owner you are in control (allegedly) – you can cut hours and reduce the wage bill when times are tough and expand your workforce when times are good - and yet they are the biggest source of worry.

Staff are where most things are likely to go wrong (they are particularly active with Sod's Law). For example, it's 6pm on a Saturday when you're fully booked with two of the team on holiday and the phone rings. It's Fred's mum saying that poor little Freddie is ill and really shouldn't work around food for 48 hours – conveniently missing the busiest shifts of the weekend and rocking-up on Monday when everyone's on their knees.

Or, as in our place in Cornwall, replace, 'is ill,' with 'surf's up,' and the net result is the same – adding in the fact that the sun's shining and the tourists will be out in their droves and we'll be busier than ever with fewer staff than on a normal day!

A vital gene for hospitality staff

Recruit staff with a 'fast' gene. By this I mean people who work smartly and efficiently and who understand the concept of fast service. If you can find people with the 'fast gene' AND the gene that means they can't have an empty hand when passing tables that need clearing, litter that needs picking up or any other array of tasks that perpetually need doing, then you're onto a winner.

The alternative is the usually empty-handed recruit with the 'slow gene' – like Tamsin who we employed one year, delightful, polite and great at delivering cold meals – usually getting the last meal set down just as the first meal is finished and ambling past tables that need clearing. Obviously she's kindly letting someone else collect the plates.

Family Values

I'm a firm believer in creating a culture at work akin to family. There will always be the mini squabbles and episodes characteristic of most families, but if you create some core values that represent your culture and management style – you won't go far wrong.

Let's face it, hospitality can be a tough industry with long hours and the chances are that many of your team will spend longer with you than they will with their partners. While it's important to get them to leave their troubles on the doorstep while they are at work, and plaster that smile on as part of the 'theatre', it's important you appreciate them and care for them into the bargain.

Trust good staff with your business

Once you've got a good team on board, share the numbers - they see a till full of money and think it's all yours. Help them see how this is not the case. Pin up the utility bills and run 'turn it off' incentives to see how they can affect the overheads. It might be worth giving them an idea of your overheads and costs, for example, VAT, corporation tax, electricity, heating, rates, wages, PAYE, national insurance, repairs, rent, trading insurance, advertising, legal fees, cleaning products, capital equipment, glasses, the list goes on. A pound earned is worth a lot less than a pound saved – a pound saved goes straight into your business pocket.

Reward

Remember to say, 'thank you', when staff have worked hard (a text message to a staff member at 1am on their way home saying 'thank you' is worth its weight in gold – it is not only polite but shows you've noticed.)

Among the best currencies for rewarding the team we found were doughnuts and Easter eggs – my husband would return from Cash and Carry with a little treat for all the team. Low cost yet highly prized!

If you do pick more structured incentive and reward schemes make sure the reward hits the button with the individual – some are motivated by money, some by thoughtful treats. The knack is to understand what will get the individual to take action to achieve it (tank rides, weekends off, Michelin starred dinners, M&S vouchers and weekends away have all featured on my list over the years).

Years ago I had a chef who was a bit random in his performance. He would jog along fine for a while and then gradually slip into bad ways – showing up late, being slapdash with the food, making a hash out of ordering. Eventually things would get so bad that I would give him a verbal or written warning – this would miraculously transform him back into a model employee! It took me ages to work out the pattern – and finally I twigged. His motivation wasn't money, or even material things, or getting on with colleagues – all he wanted was my time and to have an opportunity to talk regularly about his job and role in the business. Every time I gave him a warning he had my undivided attention to 'offload,' as we discussed him, his job and his feelings about it. Building a regular hour a month 'him' time meant we got the best out of him without all the warnings!

Staff Rules

A bit like toddler training that never ends, you need to give firm boundaries about things like cigarette breaks, staff food, amount of notice for days off and 'shift swaps' (no, you can't cover your shift as bar manager with a newly recruited 18 year old waitress). Generally with staff rules your role is to lead by example.

Cover yourself against staff being absent

Create a dish specification so if the chef does a moonlight flit someone else can pick up the pieces more easily – there is an argument that if you can read, you can cook – all cooking is following a set of instructions with a set of precisely measured ingredients!

Train as many members of the team (front and back of house) on different kitchen sections (salad prep, snacks and desserts, service). If there's a shortage or you are extra busy they can jump in and help.

View your business as an employee

Imagine you have the swankiest new Android phone, you want to bring it to work in case your kids, husband, mum needs to get hold of you and so you can make your social arrangements in your break. Are you likely to want to leave it in your coat pocket hanging where anyone can see it?

There needs to be somewhere safe to leave it, if there's not your staff member will want to keep it with them during a shift – which in turn leads to temptation to text and the possibility of being on the phone when a customer needs attention.

Create a decent environment where good members of staff want to turn up for work – and get a waiting list of good people who want to work with you, the best places all have this and can basically pick and choose great staff. Create a career progression with a clear learning path and you will hold onto staff much longer. It's a good idea to have a table on the wall in a staff only area showing each member of staff and what areas of the business they've been trained in and what industry qualifications they have obtained. It's a good motivator as staff will all want to be seen as highly competent. Try out the 'Our Team Rocks' and 'We Rock' templates at the back of the book.

Staff rule ok?

Yes chef!

Here's the question – are you the chef or are you running the business?

Can you really implement all that marketing and number crunching and still be in the kitchen? One thing's for sure, you can't do front of house and cook the food, so you will need to make a decision – if you can't stand the heat in the kitchen you will need a cook/chef.

If you decide to employ one you will need to understand - they are a quite unique breed.

Over the years I have hired chefs who are hypochondriacs, psychos (one in particular invented a girlfriend who repeatedly suffered the most dreadful disasters – car crashes, miscarriages, bereavements, weird contagious illnesses – all of which were untrue. Until we found out she didn't exist he managed to get the most extraordinary amount of compassionate leave ever!) Most of them were quite ok with chopped off fingers or third degree burns – but get a back twinge and they were off for weeks. Of course there were some ultra-professional and loyal ones – Chris and Dave you know who you are – Ben and Si too.

On the whole, chefs don't see the light of day, don't have much of a social life and have a high pressure job (I know it's not life or death but a surgeon working in a casualty department is a fair analogy). You never know in advance how many people you will have to deal with – you don't know what they'll choose or how many will come at once and they will all want immediate attention. There will be an instant judgment on the quality of your work and your reputation is on the line every single day!

Getting a good chef is vital.

Generally they fall into two camps

- Job hoppers – full of great ideas but likely to leave you in the lurch in a year's time

- Long servers – these are safe, competent and reliable and stay with you a long time. Most of us go 'phew' when we land one as it provides stability and an end to kitchen staffing crises - we can't shut the door and put up a sign 'We'll cook your dinner tomorrow because we're between chefs.' However, with long servers beware the 'roast beef baguette special syndrome'. This is when he or she gets set in their ways and the best 'special' they can come up with on a Monday is using up yesterday's roast meats in a sandwich which is hardly special or worth the (usually) inflated salary we have given them to guard against them leaving. Chef complacency and reluctance to embrace new trends can, bit by bit, destroy your business.

No-one's perfect

One of the best ways I found of getting round the shortcomings of two chefs who worked for us for a few years was to incentivise them to keep the kitchen clean with a fun bonus system. Like many dedicated chefs, this duo were hard workers but not really enamoured with implementing the cleaning rotas. After a visit from EHO where we were given a decidedly mediocre report I devised a cleaning bonus for them – it went like this:

Every cleaning task in the kitchen was listed and a number was given to it – under the fat fryers number 25, roof of the microwave number 57, seals of the dessert fridge number 13 – you get the picture. Once this was done I took two packs of cards and overwrote numbers 1 – 100 on their face (there were 100 cleaning tasks). Every Friday before evening service I shuffled the cards and got the boys to randomly choose five cards. I then 'inspected' the corresponding cleaning task to the numbers they had selected. If they all five were clean and up to standard they got a bonus. If they weren't they didn't.

The randomness of this meant that all areas had to be clean at all times – this focused their efforts enormously and made them make better use of the team too.

See chef incentive templates in chapter 7.

Osmosis Law

As an owner of a business it's helpful to think that common sense doesn't really exist and your hope that staff 'should' know things automatically is not going to work. Believing the Law of Osmosis (osmosis being a process that spontaneously transfers a solution from one side of an invisible membrane to the other) will take care of all your training needs, magically transferring your own industry knowledge and impeccable service skills into the heads of your staff, is a mistake.

Assume they don't have common sense and will need your help to get proficient in their work. Remember you will experience staff members who will do the same thing day-in, day-out, then one day do it totally differently for no apparent reason. It happens!

Golden Rule No.21

You can't do it all on your own. Tell yourself: 'I need people around me who can do the stuff I can't; my job is to help them be the best they can be.'

Hire slowly...

...fire quickly

With the fast pace of the catering world, and the fact it never sleeps, it's tempting to just take whoever applies without really thinking about the medium and long-term.

Hiring slowly, if at all possible, will help you avoid costly mistakes and 'hanging on' to someone who has clearly gone off the boil and can't be re-invigorated with training or motivation. This can have a massive detrimental effect on trade and on the morale of the rest of the team. In this instance 'half a loaf' is definitely NOT better than 'no bread.'

Ask a chef at interview to cook for you before you employ them. I don't care if you're a sandwich shop or a Michelin star restaurant – get them in for a trial.

It sounds so obvious but it took me 15 years to get to a point where I asked an interviewee to cook for me BEFORE I employed him or her.

This will tell you vital things in advance of any contract you issue.

In the early days my hubby and I employed a local lad who convinced us at interview he would be perfect for our quality Bistro-style food offer – unfortunately our hopes were dashed a few days in as we asked him to prepare a Special of the Day and he created 'Cheesy Beany Bake' - a recipe it transpired he'd gleaned from Blue Peter!

A trial food cook-off will give you a chance to check:

1. **Food** - is the food delicious? Taste is vital

2. **Temperament** - can they interact well with others in the kitchen – is he/she a
shouter – a bully or lacking presence?

3. **Working method** - is he/she a clean worker – a messy worker is hard to integrate – it costs lots in wages and breeds staff resentment in those having to clean up after him/her and may ring alarm bells for food safety?

Finding the right chef for your business is a bit like finding a partner – you have to be able to work as a team, share the same vision and core values and work through the arguments and bad times!

In Chapter 7 there is a template crib sheet to make sure you ask the right questions.

Golden Rule No.22
Chefs can be weird – get over it!

Service with a smile?

Or with a scowl?

From how your team greet customers – 'Good evening sir, madam,' 'Hi guys,' 'Wotcha, Fred,' to the way the food is delivered to your customer – silver service, self-service or somewhere in between - there are aspects of how you, and your staff, serve your customers that will improve your chances of success – whatever your style of food business.

Make sure your team understands what good service in your individual outlet looks like.

Whether it's casual and informal, make sure your team are empowered to use greetings and words appropriate to, and expected by, the customer. For example, it won't go down too well in a high-end restaurant if the staff plonk plates down with an Aussie 'Here you go, guys!'

Top Tip

When employing waiting staff, get them to understand your service culture by treating them as guests, from the greeting when they come in, to serving them food and drink, then the farewell and thank you. Ask them to note how they felt throughout the process; they may even have ideas on how things could be improved.

To understand the impact your waiting staff have on the success of your business make sure they are aware of the tiny things they do that customers notice. Ask them to put themselves in the customers' shoes and view themselves as customers do.

1. **What are your hands doing?** - be conscious of your little mannerisms – I'm a customer and I'm watching you rub your eyes, nose, mouth, ear and then using those same hands to pass me my dinner plate. You probably are a very clean person, but I simply don't want your germs on my food.

2. **Leave your hair alone** – I really don't want to see you running your hand through your hair, or tucking it behind your ears to keep it from falling forward in your face.

3. **Touchy-feely** - there is really no need for you to touch me as one of your guests. Placing your hand on someone's back to guide them to their seat is just not necessary. Contrary to popular belief, touching the customer, in an obviously non-sexual manner, doesn't build a connection or attract a better tip. A lot of people think it's plain creepy.

4. **Get off your mobile** - I don't care if you've got a moment where you can check your texts, tweets and posts, I'm the customer and without me you wouldn't have a job, so the least you can do is to be more interested in me than your mates when you're at work.

5. **Spit out your gum** - just no, no, no! Chewing gum is utterly unprofessional.

6. **Pay attention to where you place your fingers** - please don't hand me my drink with your fingers touching the rim of the glass, or leave your thumb print on my dinner.

7. **Don't sniff** - please don't arrive at the table and 'smell' a drink if you can't remember which similar looking dark liquid belongs to what customer. A more professional option is to own-up to the confusion, take the drinks back to the kitchen and start all over again.

8. **Don't lean on me** – I haven't read any rule book that says English etiquette is to always set down to the left (using left hand if possible) of an individual and clear from the right (using the right hand if possible). What I want is for you to serve me in the least obtrusive way – not leaning over me, sticking your shoulder (or worse) in my ear or friends and colleagues at my table.

9. **If you're ill, please go home** - rather than sniffling and fighting back a cough, the courteous thing to do is find someone that can switch shifts with you until you are feeling better.

10. **Don't take a cheeky taster** - you may think you are safely out of sight as you take a taste from a plate coming out of the kitchen or going back into the kitchen…you will be seen.

11. **Don't ask if everything is 'OK!'** – OK? OK is not OK! Since when is 'OK' good enough? I paid hard-earned money for this food and I want it to be the best and most delicious food your establishment can muster, not something that is 'OK' (if you were the customer, and I the server, and you asked me about a particular dish and I said, 'it's OK', would you think that's a good answer. No. You wouldn't. So using OK in a question isn't good, either).

Ask me an open-ended question, such as, 'how is your meal?' I'll respond accordingly: 'delicious' or direct you to any problems such as 'we're still waiting for the sauce,' or 'everyone's is lovely but mine's a little tough.' And if you say it – say it like you mean it and not in that glib "I couldn't care less" tone! Even if you don't mean it act like you have genuine concern or interest in my satisfaction.

12. **Bring back my change** - I know it's only 50p but, unless I tell you otherwise, please bring back every penny.

13. **Know the menu** - you don't have to have eaten everything on the menu, but you should have a good idea of the important ingredients in every dish that may affect customers (see Chapter 4 allergies) and what other people say about it, and you should be able to answer my questions about it. If you don't know the answer to a question, I would much prefer you ask someone instead of making something up or, worse, saying, 'I think so'. We don't do 'think' so. We do 'know' so. Be willing to give a recommendation, but for the love of God, don't tell me everything on the menu is a masterpiece.

14. **Tell us the specials and how much they cost** - even if there's a big sign listing the specials, it would be great if you could go over them with my friends and me. I am notorious for neglecting to look at those specials signs and missing out on good food because of it. I'm just not always that observant. So tell me about it.

15. **Smile and be polite or get a different job** - part of the job is customer service, and it's difficult to give good service if you seem like you're in a foul mood. So put on a smile! Act happy! Frankly, serving customers is theatre. You're on show, whether you like it or not. Sometimes, pretending to be happy actually improves your mood. And I promise you this: being smiley, happy and friendly will improve your tips.

16. **Listen to me and watch me** – more than 50% of communication is non-verbal - you need to know this and be bright enough to understand what I'm telling you with my non-verbal cues. If you're good at this you'll soon pick up on my vibe and understand the role I want you to play in my experience of visiting your establishment. I may want to have a laugh and a joke with you, I may want you to be invisible, I may want you to chat to me while I wait for my friend and then back off when she arrives. What I want is for you to make me feel comfortable – and this will be different every time I come in.

17. **Don't call me 'darling'** – or maybe, do call me 'darling,' it depends on circumstances: sometimes it works, sometimes it doesn't. It's easy enough to judge. I need you to speak to me in a way that doesn't embarrass me or make me feel foolish or uncomfortable.

Golden Rule No.23

The success or failure of your business is in the hands of people paid not much more than the minimum wage. Create a work culture and learning environment for your team with customer service at its core.

Profit Vampires your staff bring to the business

No.37 Bad communication

When food is returned to the kitchen because it is the wrong dish, cooked well done when it should be rare or special instructions such as 'sauce on the side' have not been followed, you are literally throwing money in the bin. While mistakes will always happen, keep them to a minimum through having proper and effective communication with the people taking the orders and the kitchen team.

I once witnessed this scenario where a wrongly delivered bangers and mash was whisked away after the gentleman had taken a bite of his sausage. The uproar continued five minutes later when another table complained that they had been served a sausage with a bite out!

Whatever happens, the food is wasted and what's worse, customers are upset. Pay particular care to a foolproof system if you have an outside area – as people will move tables and generally muck things up.

No.38 Taking food to the wrong table

Not having a table recognition system can result in ghastly mistakes!
Taking an order to the wrong table can create a horrible mess – particularly if some of the dishes are common to the two confused tables and someone decides to start nibbling before the mistake is discovered

No.39 Not promoting certain dishes

There will be certain dishes on your menu that make a busy service easier
If you have really busy sessions that put a strain on service consider promoting and training your team to 'lead' customers to dishes that are simpler to prepare to avoid waiting times getting longer. You may want to consider highlighting the low skill and high margin items that can be assembled by a semi-skilled operative quickly, allowing more meals per minute out of the kitchen.

No.40 Starting shifts at the same time

Staggering the starting time and finishing time of hourly paid staff will ensure you have cover in the busy service sessions but you won't be paying staff to twiddle their thumbs before the customers arrive.

No.41 Not creating special offers

Special offers will help drive trade to fill the quiet times.
Many food businesses are quieter than they'd like to be Monday to Thursday but wish they were twice the size at the weekends. Having an empty premises whether midweek, January/Feb or November is a wasted asset. Rent, rates and staff all still need to be paid so customers should be enticed to visit during quiet times.

Offers should be sufficiently exciting to get customers to take action. They should be low cost and have high-perceived value. Bear in mind that '10% off' is a weak promotion - it will only take cash from your bottom line, not be sufficient to drive additional footfall and may well only serve to squeeze your margins with customers who would have visited you (and paid full price) anyway.

No.42 Not having a specials board

A Specials Board is a great way of experimenting, trying new dishes and keeping things fresh for regular visitors who may have 'eaten their way' though the fixed menu. Judging the customer uptake of dishes tried out on the specials board can help you determine if they should become a regular on your main menu. Menu printing can be costly and the last thing you want is to be stuck with is having to hold ingredients (and potentially waste) for dishes that only sell once in a blue moon. A Specials Board is also a great way to optimise return from a seasonal glut or give a response to the weather.

No.44 Not controlling switch on/off

Power costs are one of the biggest overheads after rent and staff costs. Controlling these is vital to profitability so take extra care in the kitchen where the biggest outlay can be. Hot water, powerful microwaves, fryers and stoves will all contribute significantly to your fuel bills. Signpost exact times each piece of equipment should be turned on and off. For example, a fryer really only needs to be turned on ten minutes before service – not the minute chef walks in at 9.00am. The oven should be turned off the minute service has ended – not last thing before lights out.

No.43 Not training to sell

In particular not training the staff to sell short-dated/glut items
This can be done either in person by the server or with a well thought out 'chef recommends' table talker. Generally people are unsure what to order - whether this is laziness or they simply can't think what to choose when faced with a lot of options, recommending a particular dish makes it easy for them. And if that 'just happens' to be what you need to shift, it's a great way to avoid waste and maximise profit.

No.45 Not having a booking system

Whether it's a fancy-pants electronic system or a good old fashioned paper diary, you need a system. Not staggering your bookings properly or allocating the right table for bookings can have a big impact on your takings. You need to have a fool proof system for your staff to follow. If you have a restaurant with 20 tables that each seat four, but you have 20 bookings for couples, you can literally half your potential take for that day. On busy days many restaurants limit the number of 2's they will take to the number of tables that only seat two.

Staggering bookings to spread the flow of orders into the kitchen is essential – not only to avoid service issues caused by all the orders arriving at one time and chef having to go from zero meals ordered to 50 in the space of five minutes - but also to ensure you get some early bookings that will allow you to turn tables and have them available for later diners.

Top Tip:

Divide your booking diary into table slots and allocate a number against each that represents the maximum number that can sit at that table. Define the volume of orders you would like in the kitchen at any one given time. Break your booking slots into 15 minute slots.

Create a corresponding number of strike through boxes to the volume of orders you have decided upon per 15 minute slot. When a booking is taken simply strike through the appropriate number of guests – when one section is all struck through you can tell your guests '8.00 is fully booked but we have a table at 7.45 available.' Nobody will really mind but the flow of orders will be all the better and so will the service.

No.44 Not controlling switch on/off

Power costs are one of the biggest overheads after rent and staff costs. Controlling these is vital to profitability so take extra care in the kitchen where the biggest outlay can be. Hot water, powerful microwaves, fryers and stoves will all contribute significantly to your fuel bills. Signpost exact times each piece of equipment should be turned on and off. For example, a fryer really only needs to be turned on ten minutes before service – not the minute chef walks in at 9.00am. The oven should be turned off the minute service has ended – not last thing before lights out.

"Our Team Rocks" and "Customer Status Checklist"

In the template section of this book I have included a couple of summary tables I found really useful when trying to keep on top of staff training.

Our Team Rocks Basics

This is an example of how to define some of the key opening up, service and close procedure for a restaurant, bar, café – yours will be as individual as your outlet (and I suggest you compile a handbook outlining exactly what these might be). By breaking tasks down into specifics in this way helps you monitor who has been trained to do basic tasks such as cleaning the coffee machine down at the end of service, or serving wine in the restaurant. I used to use a traffic light system with red orange and green stickers marking whether someone had just started training – was halfway there or fully trained in a given procedure.

We Rock WOW!

Is a continuation of this system but focuses on some of the key service criteria (reading the 'moment' or customer's body language) that can result in your team giving some WOW! Service – creating some magic moments and memorable service your customers will love.

Customer Status Checklist

I found this really useful to keep on top of table service and make sure the team didn't miss any sales opportunities. Having a written reference point for all staff and management to see (we had pads of these printed off and kept at the waiting station) meant that at a glance we could see who was waiting – when a table might become free, and where each table was with the course of their meal. I'm sure there are electronic equivalents now (ResDiary for example) but the principle is sound from this old-fashioned checklist. Often bookings would be made for one time and customers not sit down until much later because they were chatting at the bar – the checklist overview was a great help to manage potential flash points during service.

6 It's all about you!

Seven characteristics of successful food operators

What separates good operators from the wannabes?

These seven characteristics:

1. **Responsibility** - good operators wake up every day and say: 'The buck stops here'

2. **Focus** - good operators know the difference between time wasted and time well spent

3. **Inner strength** - good operators have an unshakeable inner belief that their business will succeed

4. **Specific aims** - good operators create SMART goals

5. **Vision** - good operators get out more!

6. **Perspective** - good operators have a true set of core values

7. **Emotion** - good operators take a detached view of their business

In some of my presentations I often ask the audience of restaurateurs, publicans and chefs this simple question: 'What's stopping your business from growing?'

The response is usually a murmur of grumbles about the Government; the economic climate; red tape and complying with endless rules and regulations; tax; staff issues; competition - and the occasional hard luck story.

The problem I have with this response is that, while there may be exceptions, these 'reasons' that people cite that are holding them back from success affect every business in the country. Every single one, without exception – and yet there are many examples of extraordinarily successful food operations that have grown and flourished against the same gloomy backdrop.

You only have to look at operations like Giraffe – which started with one restaurant and a 'vision' sixteen years ago. Having achieved massive growth during some of the hardest economic years ever, it was acquired by Tesco in 2013 for a cool £50 million. This clearly demonstrates that successful businesses can flourish whatever the climate. What really counts is attitude.

1. 'The Buck Stops Here'

The answer to my earlier question if your business isn't growing as you'd like it to is:

'Me.'
'I'm stopping my business from succeeding.'
'I'm in charge.'
'It's down to me.'

US President Harry S. Truman had a sign with this inscription on his desk indicating that he didn't pass the buck to anyone else but accepted personal responsibility for the way the country was governed.

The phrase originated from 'passing the buck,' coined in poker games where a buckskin handled knife was passed around the table as a marker of who had the responsibility for dealing. When the dealer's turn was done, he passed the buck, or responsibility, to the next man.

Speaking to food business operators over the last 30 years, it is clear to me that there is one thing and one thing only that marks the successful operators from those that are simply 'getting by,' or just about scraping a living – and that's the responsibility they take for their actions.

Culpability; responsibility; liability; accountability – whatever word you use, it is the distinguishing quality that gives a person the strength of character to accept that the buck well and truly stops with them.

Getting out of the blame culture is the first thing a restaurant owner needs to do if he or she is to succeed. It will simply hold you back if you cling on to the, 'Oh yes, this place would be great if it wasn't for the rents I'm charged,' or 'that chain restaurant a few doors down can do things so much cheaper than us, they take all our business.'

The thing is - who signed the lease? Err … hello, wasn't that you? Presumably no-one forced your hand and shouldn't you have checked your numbers stacked-up and the business model worked before you signed? Had you thought it through? Did you have a realistic business plan?

Bleating on about problems further down the line, when the cracks start to show is no way forward – you are where you are today because of the actions you took yesterday.

Golden Rule No.24

Accept that whatever happens in your business, good and bad, is down to you. Repeat this daily mantra: 'I can't run it successfully by ducking my responsibilities or by blaming anyone else...the buck stops with me.'

2. Time well-spent

There are 1,440 glorious minutes in every day

Much has been written by the business gurus about time management and the fact that successful business owners, whether in hospitality or in any other business, have the same number of minutes in their days as we mere mortals do in ours. And yet they are able to build empires in their lifetime whereas we may build a sandcastle of two.

Four things to make the most of your time:

Never let a day go by

Putting off till tomorrow what could be done today is a maxim that haunts me from my childhood – and yet there are some things that could and indeed should be put off till tomorrow and the business will be all the better for it!

I personally take enormous inspiration from Ben Hunt-Davis who won Olympic Gold at the Sydney Olympics in 2000 as part of the Men's Rowing Eight. In his book *'Will It Make The Boat Go Faster?'* he identified how creating that one simple question proved to be the peg onto which he and the team could hang their actions, manage their time and focus on what really mattered to become gold medal winners.

Every day is filled with challenges and (in hospitality in particular) firefighting situations that demand our immediate attention – the drains are blocked; so-and-so has called in sick; the sun's out and we are understaffed; we sold out and need more supplies. What Ben and his team did – every time they were faced with a situation that might throw their training off course was to apply the 'will it make the boat go faster?' question – if the answer was 'yes' – they did it – if 'no' they didn't.

This really manifested itself at the Olympics themselves when they were the first team EVER to refuse to attend the opening ceremony.

Asking the question – made them realise that NO! Would they normally march for miles – over a five hour period the night before a really important race? Of course not – so why do it at the opening ceremony the night before the most important race they had trained four years for! It would obviously seriously impact on their concentration and fitness. Having the question – made prioritising the action really easy.

Such razor-sharp clarity is what's needed when deciding what really should have a call on our time – and what should really be parked!

In hospitality, the trick to knowing what should be done today and what can wait is prioritisation. I have two lists and the question 'will it help me get and keep more customers?'

List A contains the goals I set to increase trade and profitability. Basically the criterion here is: 'Will doing xxxx (detail of task) help me get nearer to my profitability goals?' If the answer is yes then it deserves a place on list A

List B is the day-to-day stuff that keeps me in business 'the doing' (staff rotas, cooking, serving, cleaning and trouble shooting)

For example, if my goal for May was to increase sales of coffees by £400, I would break down the number of daily sales I need which translates to six cups per day.

My List A would include tasks that would help me increase sales such as:

- Creating a staff incentive to increase coffee sales
- Organising/holding a training session to introduce the incentive
- Creating a special offer on coffee and cake
- Creating marketing materials for the coffee and cake special offer
- Creating an email campaign to promote coffee
- Planning coffee related facebook posts and tweets to promote coffee
- Organising a coffee 'event' involving suppliers and a barista demonstration
- Setting questions for a coffee facts table-talker competition

These tasks would take priority over the day-to-day tasks as they are fundamental to the success of the sales goal.

Block your tasks – be ruthless with your time!

It's incredible how much time we waste switching between tasks in a busy workplace environment. No more so than in hospitality where there always seems to be a backdrop of panics and crisis – with staff not showing-up, bits of equipment breaking down and unexpected rushes of custom.

Constant interruptions can steal your time (do you really need to see this salesman right now – simply because he's in the area and thought he'd 'drop in') and mean that you never quite get round to the really important stuff on your List A – the stuff that will drive your business forward.

An easy way of managing this is through blocking your time and ruthlessly sticking to it. Rather than making a phone call or sending an email as it occurs to you - set aside a period of time daily when you'll do just calls or emails.

Keep an hour a day absolutely clear (no interruptions) to tackle tasks on your List A. When you write it in your diary you don't need to know exactly what you're going to tackle – just that this block of time can ONLY be spent on A list tasks.

Delegate your weaknesses to someone else's strengths

You simply can't do it all yourself – if you try you'll crash and burn or stay really small. You need to be able to hand over tasks to others – ideally the stuff you don't like to do, or find difficult. Make sure when you brief others with tasks that you don't fall foul of the 'Osmosis Law' (see Chapter 5) or you will be frustrated when they don't deliver what you want

Be strict on daily disciplines

This is the really, really difficult one. But it's a fact that a common trait of successful operators is their personal and professional effectiveness. In fact one of the best business books I've read is 'The Seven Habits of Highly Effective People' by Steven Covey. In this book Steven explores how our daily habits and unconscious patterns constantly express our character and produce our effectiveness, or ineffectiveness, in everything we do – including our business life. Good and bad habits will ultimately affect our success. Things such as blocking out periods of time for tackling tasks on your List A, when they become a regular habit, will make us more effective and more successful. On the flip side, habits that allow us to be distracted and allow trivial tasks to take priority will mean sales growth will be more elusive.

Golden Rule No.25

Managing your time effectively and prioritising tasks is central to the success or failure of your business.

3. Unshakeable inner belief that your business will succeed

Part of the basic training for all British soldiers and top athletes is that when they are absolutely knackered and in agony – a forced march, a long sprint - they are taught that when they think they can't go any further, the truth is, 'yes, they can': their body is capable of going on, but their mind is giving up. Therefore, all top soldiers and athletes train their minds as much as they train their bodies.

Your mind-set, whether you're in the SAS, the British Olympic Team or running your own business, makes the difference between success or failure. Your attitude is the driving force.

You must not adopt a lightweight responsibility and have a 'playing at it' or 'I really want my business to succeed' frame of mind. You must have a genuine vision, backed by sound commercial savvy, and an absolute conviction that whatever is thrown at you – and it usually hits you at the very worst time – you will adapt, improvise and overcome. You will succeed. It is not a 'want' but an utter faith in one's own ability to make a success of one's vision. It's a 'my business WILL succeed' mind-set.

JD Wetherspoon – one of the most successful and profitable newcomers to the licensed hospitality sector in recent times did not start to show a profit until 1984 – five years after Tim Martin founded the company.

Up against a marketplace full of scorn, derision – and even some who wanted him to fail publicly - Tim Martin forged on with an enduring inner belief in his vision of what a pub should be.

Tim, as a young entrepreneur in 1976, had a vision which allegedly stemmed from an article about George Orwell in the Evening Standard from 40 years earlier describing his perfect pub – no music so that customers could talk freely, selling cheap and nutritious food, serving its draught beer in pewter tankards, and where the friendly barmaids know your name (and they're always glad you came).

Orwell called his dream boozer The Moon Under Water and Martin was inspired to name and style his first establishments after Orwell's dream. There are still 14 Moons, but the vast majority of Tim's pubs owe their names to a hybrid of homage and cheek.

The JD bit is taken supposedly from JD 'Boss' Hogg – not one of the pigs in Animal Farm, but the sheriff in the TV series The Dukes of Hazzard. Wetherspoon was the surname of a geography teacher Martin encountered at a New Zealand school, who not only assured the boy Martin that he would never amount to anything much, but was also a teetotaller! If only that teacher knew what he'd inspired – more than 800 pubs with his name on the front! Guess who had the last laugh!

This inner belief shown by Martin and other successful operators (Jamie Oliver and Gordon Ramsay spring to mind) has to be personal. When you dig a bit deeper with any successful businessperson who's made it from nothing – there is always a back-story that reveals grit and determination at the very core of their journey to success.

This inner belief has to be genuine. It has to be sincere.

If somewhere at the back of your mind you've got a 'cop-out'– a Plan B – an 'if this doesn't work, I'll do something else,' – then the chances are you will be doing something else.

 Golden Rule No.26
Failures along the way are inevitable and will speed your journey to success. Tell yourself 'ultimate failure is not an option.' Adopt a positive mental approach even on the bad days. Think of Henry Ford's quote: 'Whether you think you can or think you can't - you're probably right.'

4. Create SMART Goals

Don't switch off – this really matters and isn't just a regurgitation of all those self-help business books!

In 2003 we had the following sign on our kitchen wall:

"We want to be recognised by the licensed-trade industry to be the best. We want you all (our staff) to share in this recognition. In 18 months' time (May 2004) we want to own a free house."

In 2003 we won the industry's top accolade "UK Licensee of the Year" and in Feb 2004 we purchased our free house – going on to sell it three years later for a £1m more than we bought it for.

I sincerely don't believe this was 'coincidence'.

There is no question in my mind that by creating smart goals and writing them down for others to see, you have a much better chance of achieving them. I'm always amazed at how few people actually do this.

Creating SMART goals (Specific, Measurable, Achievable, Realistic and Time-Accountable) every year will definitely help you move your business forward and keeping them updated them throughout the year will keep you on track and allow you to respond to shifts and changes in focus.

The successful business person almost always does this. It's important to point out that just writing them down seldom leads to getting them accomplished. Accountability is what gets them accomplished. That's why you need others to see your smart goals.

Put simply – without a SMART goal – you might as well put your life savings into lottery tickets and keep your fingers crossed!

5. Get out more - learn more

There is nothing as bad for your business as getting 'stuck' – working so hard in your business to the exclusion of everything else. Never taking a day out, never eating out or staying away, never taking a training course or learning a new skill.

When we bought our place in North Cornwall the whole town of pubs and restaurants seemed 'stuck', with no idea what was going on in other parts of the country or world. I'm sure there were a few exceptions, but the majority were stuck in the 'budget' mentality – thinking all ingredients should be bought as cheaply as possible – with no emphasis on quality, while just 30 miles along the coast people were happily parting with £25 - £35 for freshly prepared fish and chips. They were still frying off frozen battered cod (remarkable as we were literally 200 yards from the sea) and garnishing their dishes a la 80's – complete with iceberg lettuce, grated carrot and mustard and cress!

Given these circumstances our 'worldlier vision' meant that when we dropped the cheap ingredients for local produce and sprinkled in a bit of rocket to the garnish we cleaned up! The point being, I would imagine that the furthest most of the restaurant owners in the town had been to lately was Launceston (15 miles), and were quite oblivious to all the great new trends emerging across the country.

Getting out and about means you get to experience new ideas, market trends customer preferences. Every time you get out of your business you should be able to find at least one good idea you can copy, adjust and use in your outlet.

I have to this day a 'swipe' file in which I keep other peoples menus, flyers, websites, Facebook pages, anything I see and think – 'I like that' or 'I could do that'. Copy, adapt, deploy that's my motto.

The other limiter on your business is you – if you stop learning that is. Einstein is famously quoted as defining madness as doing the same thing over and over and expecting a different result - learning new skills and better business methods is at the heart of avoiding this sort of madness.

Put another way, why does school stop the minute you get the keys to your business? When you first went to school you couldn't read or write – now you can.

You went to school and sat in a classroom and learned how to do it, practised what you learned and got better and better at doing it. The same principles apply to running a food business – and yet so many business owners spend time practising without getting the learning bit!

6. Define your core values

This is important if you are working in your pub, café, restaurant, hotel or sandwich shop as a 'pair', whether with your husband, wife, civil partner, friend, parent, son or daughter. Let's face it, sustaining happy and stable long-term relationships can be a hard ask at the best of times – chuck into the mix the long hours, fatigue, stress flash points of a busy service and alcohol all associated with the hospitality industry and it's not surprising things often end in tears.

Key to the success of a partnership or family-run business is sharing the same set of core values. A bit like the 'Will it make the boat go faster?' question, it pays to ask yourself 'remind me again why am I doing this?'

If you are working as a pair your reasons need to be the same and in the same priority order.

For example:

His reasons: To make money, to be a 'somebody' – well known and respected, to have a busy social life
Her reasons: To be able to work around the kids, to have security, to be together as a couple at work

This is seriously never going to work as a business partnership as there will be constant stresses pulling them in different directions – he may want to spend time socialising with the customers while she would prefer to be in the park with the kids.

If you both come from a hospitality background this helps enormously too. Many partnerships founder where one partner comes into the industry from a 9-5 background while the other knows the deal!

Now I'm not saying here that you need to share exactly the same skill sets and characteristics – in fact it is a strong partnership where individual's skills complement each other: one partner with an eye for detail, good with numbers, methodical, well planned and able to prioritise, will be well complemented by a flamboyant, sociable partner with big ideas, clear vision and entrepreneurial qualities. What I'm saying is the core of the partnership needs to be driven by the same common personally held value. Such as: to provide a supportive and caring home for the kids or to create the best fast food in Croydon (and make money don't forget!)

When you both share this common value and you are up against making a tricky decision you will find the answer much simpler to make. For example asking 'Will spending a fortune on fancy tables and chairs help make our fast food operation the best in Croydon?' vs 'Will working seven days a week without a break help create a supportive and caring home for the kids"?

Having a clear and well communicated set of core values helps create a great work culture for your team too. It also benefits relationships and makes it easy to make decisions.

7. Develop detached vision

Try and look at your business dispassionately, as if you were just about to buy it. What would you change first?

Make a list of all the things you would do with your new business – now ask yourself – why aren't we doing these things anyway?

Way back in the nineties, we had created a 'restaurant extension' which had rather evolved and didn't quite match in with the rest of the building and décor. Rather than keep 'patching it up' we looked dispassionately at the business – and realised that the first thing anyone buying the place would do, would be a cosmetic makeover. We undertook a mini refurbishment – and watched our turnover soar!

Look to the future – what will your business look like three years from now? Who and what needs to be in place? What money do you need to invest? Start this process now rather than play catch-up.

If when you look forward you see yourself with a small group of restaurants, now is the time to start recruiting a team with good management skills that will help you manage these as they come on board, now is the time to introduce systems to ensure consistency of product and profit as the company expands, now is the time to put in place effective training programs to ensure continuity of service standards.

Top Tip

When you go on holiday – even if it's just to the Isle of Wight for the day – ask yourself 'If when I get back I were just taking over my business for the first time – what are the three things I would change straight away.' The clarity of thought this gives is extraordinary.

For example if you know in your heart that your enormous menu is at the root of your slow service issues. If you detach your attachment and imagine you were just taking over this business with an unruly menu – you'd chop it down in size and focus on some core dishes to prevent your team struggling through chaotic service over and over.

The ultimate secret to success?

There is no secret – successful people work bloody hard!

As touched on above, the hospitality entrepreneur needs to be just like the Olympic athlete seen receiving a Gold Medal for the best performance in the world. The 'quick fix/fast buck,' mentality will say, 'it's ok for them they've got a talent.' The truth is that they have trained day-in, day-out for years, giving up the 'norms' of social life, always eating the right foods, turning down parties and booze, starting at 4am and finishing late into the night, every day pushing their bodies beyond the pain threshold in pursuit of their Gold.

It's not really about talent, but about dedication and sacrifice. The only talent that comes into it is the talent of self-believe and determination to win.

Matthew Syed in his book *'Bounce'* (a great read – Matthew, an international table-tennis champion, explores the true nature of talent. He debunks many myths: that we can be born brilliant; that we are restricted by our genetic makeup and that our backgrounds matter). Matthew believes that a combination of thousands of hours of practice, making lots of mistakes, an ability to push the boundaries and learn from failure (the best figure skaters are those that attempt jumps, fall over and attempt again), combined with sheer hard work are guaranteed to bring success – far more so than talent. There is no quick fix, there is no short cut and you can't harvest a crop if you didn't sow the seeds.

In hospitality there is no 'one big thing' that will make a successful restaurateur. There is a path of sacrifice and compromise (family times, evenings, weekends, summer holidays, friendships), there are long hours and hard physical work, there are risks and frustrations.

But like the Olympic athlete there is that glorious and indescribable feeling of utter satisfaction – having given thousands of people fantastic special occasions, food and enjoyment - the stuff that defines our lives. Running a food operation is like having the most brilliant party, night after night after night. In hospitality we sell not just food, but good times and fun.
We make memories.

Golden Rule No.27

Do a thousand little things absolutely the best you can, no detail is too small, work bloody hard at it and have a stack of fun along the way.

CaterCost

I said at the start I am 100% dedicated to making chefs happier and food businesses more profitable. Chefs I know are happiest when they are freed to do what they do best – create amazing food. This means that if they can be unconstrained from red tape and calculations, then that would be a good thing and should make them happier.

That's why CaterCost cloud software was born. To free chefs and business owners from the hassle of spreadsheets and calculators and to provide a quick and easy way to create fully costed recipe and dish specifications on demand.

Dish specifications are at the very core of a well-run catering kitchen. A dish spec is simply a formula for creating a plate of food consistently, a bit like a recipe, but with costs attached. Our world is filled with recipe books – the top twenty Christmas books always include at least ten or more from celebrity chefs publishing their latest bunch of recipes. Just as these recipes are formulas for anyone who isn't a celebrity chef to replicate a dish, a dish specification is no different – if (heaven forbid) chef got hit by a bus, or did a moonlight flit to Bolivia, the presence of dish specifications for every line on the menu (in essence a set of instructions) will protect the business from any fallout while a replacement chef is found.

The shocking fact is that an estimated 98% of independent operators are running their food businesses without this vital template.

Without a dish specification it is really hard to intelligently handle the new food labelling laws regarding 14 allergens contained in food (EU Food Information for Consumers 1169/2011). There needs to be a reference point for business to comply – running to ask chef every time will not cut the mustard when the EHO come to check. CaterCost allows the user to check allergens against each supplied ingredient and tracks that ingredient through sub-recipes, recipes, dishes and menus – so even a drop of Worcester Sauce (Allergen 'fish' from anchovies) in a sauce will show up. Leaving much less room for error.

CaterCost key features

Why do CaterCost users like it so much?

1. You can easily create fully costed dish specifications with allergen flags and nutritional info.

2. You can create fully costed sub-recipes that sit below the main dishes with allergen flags and nutritional info. When a price changes this will flow through to all sub-recipes effortlessly.

3. You can easily monitor menu performance with profitability alerts and theoretical profit prediction for every menu. Most businesses see an uplift in profits of 4%+

4. You can simply display nutritional and allergen info via smart phone.

5. You will find it uber user-friendly because it has a really user-friendly design - above and beyond all the functionality this is probably the key to success. Most chefs are using it every day to create dish specs for the daily specials – and because it is quick and simple to do.

I think we've all experienced at some time or another the lure of shiny system that appear so integrated and clever that they would even make a cup of tea...and then realised that they are indeed too big, too flash and have a whole lot of functionality we will never use. CaterCost puts user-friendliness above everything else – what gets used works, what sits idle and shiny is of no value to the business.

So that's why CaterCost works – it is designed specifically with the independent sector in mind – and works really well with groups of businesses such as pubs – who unless they are a managed chain, tend to keep the diversity of non- standardised menus, allowing their chefs to add special dishes and utilise local produce and suppliers at outlet level, but still want accuracy and control of margins.

So here we are:

You've read my book,

You've picked up a few tips how to tweak your profitability,

Maybe now is the time to get your dish specification licked and try out CaterCost for free?

Visit **www.catercost.com** and take the free trial and see just how easy it is to add to your bottom line this year.

Good luck.

7 Templates and success blueprints

Chef interview questions

Questions you may find useful in interview for a new chef once you have covered off the basics - these probe a bit deeper

1. Why do you want to leave your current job?

What you don't want to hear is:

- Because the hours are shit
- Because the boss is a tyrant and I can't stand him/her
- Because the kitchen is rubbish
- Because the money is crap

What we're looking for in an answer is someone who is not going to use this question as an opportunity to bad mouth their current position as this person will be prone to 'unscrewing the leg of the stool.' In other words a blame culture of 'it's not my fault' – which undermines the offer they are preparing.

The nearest to a perfect answer is 'to be honest I wasn't looking for a change but I heard about this vacancy and it sounds like an exciting opportunity and an ideal match for my skills.'

2. 'I see you are on a month's notice – would you be able to start sooner?'

The only acceptable answer here involves a combination of working notice and accrued holidays. However tempting to fill a vacancy quickly, anyone prepared to leave their currant boss in the lurch for pastures new – will be prepared to do the same to you – and rest assured your turn will come. If building loyalty is important to you this guy is not for you.

3. 'Can you tell me a joke?'

Particularly revealing of character and sense of humour. Filthy jokes are acceptable in the right place (back of house) but the main thing is you will get an indication of how easily this person will interact with staff and customers – and how they will fit in.

4. 'Who do you admire and why?'

Again – this question gets to the person beneath the interview façade. I once had someone tell me two people he admired were his best mate (because he could drink 12 pints of lager and still drive home) and his Mum (because she cooked for him and washed and ironed his clothes). This guy was 29 and applying for the role of bars manager! I don't think so!

5. 'What's your favourite food to cook?'

Pot Noodle is not an acceptable answer unless you are a Pot Noodle bar. Match your prospective chef's passions to your desired menu.

6. 'Which chef would you choose as your mentor?'

This will reveal if there is any underlying passion behind their chosen career – if they see their job as simply a wage packet it will be revealed here. If they give a good answer it's an indication your menu will never be short of fresh new ideas.

7. 'What things do you not like to do?'

Everyone has things in their job description they like less than others – however if you are recruiting a FOH person and they reveal they can't stand moaning customers – or you are recruiting a chef who hates cleaning down – it may flag problems. People are often caught off guard by this question and an honest revelation is the result.

8. 'Tell me about a specific accomplishment that you're most proud of.'

There is no greater indicator of future success than past performance.

9. 'Tell me when something didn't go well.'

Hospitality is an industry where things frequently go wrong – against the backdrop of being in full view of the public at all times. An ability to overcome adversity and think on one's feet is a real asset. If candidates point the finger, blame others, go negative on a former employer or speak as an individual rather than a team player – alarm bells should ring.

customer Profile questions

Name

Sex   Age

What do they do all day? ☛	Hang out	Work as a tradesman	Watch Jeremy Kyle	Part-time office work
	Work as a manager	Work – self employed	Look after the kids	Women's Institute
	Student	Retired	Work in a shop	Professional Lawyer/Banker
	High flyer – IT consultant	Play sport	Full time work Hairdresser	Other SPECIFY

What paper do they read? ☛   Sun   Star   Telegraph   Mail   Express   Times   Guardian   Mirror   Independent   Hello/OK   Don't read one

What sport do they play? ☛	Football	Cycling	Rugby	Tennis
	Gym	Golf	Cricket	Boxing
	Running	Keep Fit	Swimming	Squash /Ski
	Don't play any	Watersports/surfing	Other SPECIFY	

What sport do they follow? ☛	Football	Rugby	Golf	Tennis
	Motor Racing	Horse Racing	Gymnastics	Cricket
	Wrestling	Boxing	Athletics	Tiddlywinks
	Curling	Chess	Don't follow any sport	Winter sports

Where do they shop for food? ☛   Lidl   Waitrose   Tesco   Aldi   Sainsburys   Local shops   Co-op   Asda   Farmers Markets   Online

What do they drink? ☛	Cask Ale	Don't Drink Alcohol	Lager	Premium Lager
	Spirits	Wine	Shots	Cider
	Flavoured beers/ciders	Mixers	Teas and coffees	Other SPECIFY

What is their favourite food? ☛	Burger	Kebab	Healthy fresh organic food	Meat and two veg
	Curry	Fish and chips	Vegetarian	Salad
	Steak	Roast dinner	Gourmet food	Pie
	Pizza	Chips	Pudding	Top quality locally sourced
	Fried breakfast	Pasta	Fresh Fish	Anything with chips

What do they do in their spare time?	Loafing	Knitting	Reading	Cooking
If they use the internet what for? ☛	Facebook and Xbox	Drinking	Walking the dog	Other SPECIFY
	Shopping	Facebook and Twitter	Banking	Emails
	Research	Naughty stuff	TV	Sport

Are they health conscious? ☛	Yes/ No			
Who do they hate? ☛	Tories	Ukip	Lefties	Taxman
	Local Authorities	Police	Scroungers	Parents
	Criminals	Immigrants	Jeremy Clarkson	Other SPECIFY
Who do they love? ☛	Spouse/ family	Bruce Forsyth	Their football team	Celebs
	Their mates	The Queen	Jeremy Clarkson	Other SPECIFY

What car do they drive? ☛   Ford   Peugeot   BMW   Merc   Clapped-out heap   Van   Vauxhall   Renault   Other SPECIFY

Where do they go on hols? ☛	Nowhere	Margate or Blackpool	Spain	Europe
	Thailand	Jamaica	USA	French Alps

195

Lifetime Value of a customer

CUSTOMER NAME
X

Average sale of CUSTOMER X	A	£
Number of sales per year to CUSTOMER X	B	£
Number of years CUSTOMER X stays with you	C	
Income per year from CUSTOMER X (A x B)	D	£
Income from CUSTOMER X in his or her buying lifetime (C X D)	E	£
Number of new customers CUSTOMER X brings you	F	
Average spend of new customers CUSTOMER X has brought you	G	£
Number of visits per year by new customers CUSTOMER X has brought you	H	
Annual income from new customers CUSTOMER X has brought you (F x G x H)	I	£
Number of years new customers stay with you (CUSTOMERS X has bought you)	J	
Lifetime value of customers customer X brings you (I x J)	K	£
TOTAL lifetime value of a customer X (K + E)		£

Use the waiting table customer status tick list to make sure you don't miss any service touch points or sales opportunities through poor communication or waiting staff forgetfulness.

Recipe Costing sheet

Recipe Name

Recipe Description

Batch size

Portion size

No of portions per batch

Dish Composition

Item	Qty	Unit	Cost £
		TOTAL COST	

Dish costing sheet

Dish Name
_____

Dish Description
_____

Dish Composition

Item	Qty	Unit	Cost £
	TOTAL COST		

Desired Gross Profit	
100 - Desired Gross Profit	**A**
(Cost divided by **A**) x 100	**B**
B x 1.2 = Retail Price	£

Menu writing **checklist**

✓ **Layout** – optimise sales of your most profitable lines by placing them in the 'hot spots'

✓ **Sections** – make it easy for your customers to find what they're looking for

✓ **Sub-headings** – because people read sub-headings more than they read the detail

✓ **Dish descriptions** – sum up what the dish is e.g. 'Ham Egg and Chips'

✓ **Words to elaborate** – describe what a customer will get on his plate e.g. 'Dry cured Wiltshire ham served with triple-cooked chips and free range eggs'

✓ **Added value** – is there a place to add 'provenance', 'personality', paint a 'picture'?

✓ **Font type** - keep it simple and legible. Can it be read in low lighting?

✓ **Dish supersizing** – offer a wow factor

✓ **Dish premiumisation** – great for adding value and increasing spend

✓ **Build-a-dish** – fun interaction and engagement with the customer

✓ **Healthy options** – displaying Kcals and nutritional information can increase sales

✓ **Special offers** – use these as a draw to fill the quiet times

✓ **Advertise** – if there is any space left blank, why not use it to promote other aspects of the business (accommodation, summer BBQs, forthcoming events). It's a great marketing spot

Everyone reads the menu!

Customer Status checklist

Table	Booking Name	No. of Guests	Time Expected	Time Arrived + Sat	Menu Given & Explained	Drinks Ordered & Water Taken	Food Order Taken	Bread	Cutlery	Starters Time	Additional Drinks Offered	Main Course Time	Additional Drinks Offered	Dessert Menu Given	Dessert Order + Dessert Wine	Dessert Time	Liquors & Coffee	Bill Given	Paid

45 Marketing Tips to promote *your business*

The more of these you have supporting your business – the stronger your business will be.

Search Engine Optimisation tabs, labels and keywords in your website will help search engines position you on page one.

Google Pay Per Click paid for advertising on Google searches is one way to drive traffic to your site – it works by you bidding on key words that a user might be searching for – e.g. fish restaurant in Birmingham, if you have sufficient budget to bid for the keywords your ad will appear at the top of the page or down the left hand side

Billboards when Richard Reed, Adam Balon and Jon Wright, founders of Innocent Smoothie, wanted to get their product into Tesco, it is rumoured that they found out where the chief buyer lived and secured a billboard hoarding on the buyer's route to work. This was a big investment from their small budget, and they kept their ad there for a fortnight. This corresponded with a direct marketing campaign which eventually opened the door for them. The perception from the Tesco buyer was that the company was much bigger than they really were – they assumed a national billboard campaign – they didn't know it was just one!

Facebook setting up a business page is really easy and a great way to get your regulars to interact with you and build loyalty. Useful features include 'check in' which lets customers friends know where they are and invitation to events which can be sent directly to anyone who likes your page.

Twitter carry on the banter and conversation even when your customers have left the building. Use this platform to drive traffic to new things on your website, YouTube, blogs and Facebook pages.

Linked In if you have a corporate or businessy customer base, this is a great place to make strategic contacts that will promote your offer.

Pinterest pictures of happy customers and lovely food – this is a great platform to show off your best assets.

Newspaper your local rag or the National Press will reach your target audience – wherever possible try and get editorial rather than a paid for ad. A compromise is Advertorial where you pay for an ad but get to write an interesting piece to promote your business too.

Broadcast media Local radio can be a really effective way of getting your message out there. Pick time slots that are appropriate for your target market.

General e-mail marketing everyone's inbox is a bit congested these days. Make sure your beautifully crafted email actually gets read with an imaginative subject line: 'This month's Newsletter' is guaranteed to be ignored. "Oops you weren't meant to get that" on the other hand will get them clicking 'open' like crazy!

Database building make it part of every day to find opportunities for you and your team to build your customer database.

45 Marketing Tips to promote your business

Blogs - short for weblog these are a popular way of adding value to your target audience by giving insights into things of interest to them. It's also a great place for a rant or to establish yourself as a 'character' or industry 'expert'.

Videos the accessibility of YouTube (one of the biggest search engines too) and the ease of shooting footage on smart phones makes this a 'no brainer' for promoting aspects of your business that lend themselves to being seen rather than described.

Google Places for Business promote your business for free by creating a profile on Google Places for Business. Not only will you appear on the right hand side of page one on Google searches but you will have 200 words to describe your business, upload photos, videos and publish upcoming events. Your customers can leave reviews here too.

Tracking numbers having a specific phone number (these are readily available from call management companies and most will give you local codes – your phone line is set exactly as now but you purchase additional phone numbers – they simply sit on top of your existing phone line and your staff answer the phone in exactly the same way) for every piece of marketing – particularly that ad in the paper – ask them to call you as the call to action and the measure the number of responses.

Auto responders scheduling emails you want to send using an automated auto-responder is a great use of your time – it can be done once and then sits pinging out emails reminding your customers you're out there – particularly if they haven't visited for a while.

Direct mail although a little expensive with postage, these can be very effective – everyone loves to get a letter – particularly if it's not a bill and not overtly salesy and contains a great offer!

Business cards what you say on your business card is important – stand out from the rest with a photo and an amusing strap line.

Websites 97% of customers search online before they visit and a huge proportion do so on a mobile device (make sure your site is mobile friendly). If you're not on the web they will find your competition instead.

Articles can you write articles for your local publications – even if it's just the parish magazine or Neighbourhood Watch newsletter? It will get your name (and so the name of the business) out there.

Squeeze pages if you use Google PPC it's worth investing in a single web page that makes your prospective customer feel like they've arrived at just the right place (your web site doesn't always do this). For example, if you are using PPC to encourage people to book Mother's Day – your squeeze page should only talk about Mother's Day. Having some kind of voucher or offer or special privilege on the page that your prospective customer has to leave their details to get the benefit, will help increase your database.

Texts use sparingly as the world of texting is still the single most read of all the cyberspace platforms and you don't want to bombard your customers and make them block you. Texting is great for getting people to take immediate action – for example if you see your bookings are low tonight – text out a really keen promotion to fill those gaps NOW!

45 Marketing Tips to promote
your business

Newsletters e-news or printed, these will help build loyalty and promote events.

Referrals you probably need take no action to get these – if your customers are happy they will tell their friends – simple as!

Events these help you fill the quieter times, create interest and persuade customers to visit more frequently. Keep things fresh and stop customers being bored.

Flyers the traditional advertising method for many – make sure your message doesn't get drowned in the text, ensure you drop to the right target market and that you have some kind of redemption to measure success – typically a 3% response is considered good – so it can prove expensive!

Sponsorship aligning yourself with, and gaining exposure from, a good cause, sports team or school and sponsoring something they do in the public domain is a great way of gaining exposure. Choose something that matches your customer demographic for maximum impact!

Reactivate past customers you can only really do this if you have collected the contact data in the first place – but sometimes customers who haven't been to you for a while need a nudge to remind them to pop in.

Loyalty cards rewarding customers for frequent purchasing is a great way to build loyalty and increase frequency of visit.

Facebook Ads these are a really simple and powerful way to increase your page likes or attract people to your site. Perfect for the hospitality industry as people on Facebook are generally in 'leisure mode."

Testimonials who better to promote your business than existing happy customers. Make it part of your daily routine to encourage them to give testimonials you can use on your web site and to post nice things on review sites such as Trip Advisor.

Offers imaginative and compelling offers will encourage new customers through your doors. Make sure they have high-perceived value to the customer whilst having a low cost to you.

Clothing putting your logo on your staff uniform will give out a professional impression and reinforce your brand. If your T-shirts are attractive they can become 'merchandise' that your loyal customers will enjoy wearing too. Phil at the Farmers Boy Inn in Gloucestershire has his shirts branded beautifully with the initials FBI – the American tourists love them!

Signage everywhere you can, use signage to make it easy for your customers to find you.

Magazines whether it's a parish mag or a postcode selective mag – if your target customers read it – you should be in it!

Books entries in "Good Food" type guides are worth their weight in gold – don't assume they will 'discover' you. Make it your mission to get your customers to recommend you.

Chef Performance Incentive Scheme

How the bonus system works:

Following a review/appraisal where areas for improvement have been identified, these areas for improvement are transposed into specific tasks that will contribute to an improvement in a specific failing. For example, if kitchen hygiene standards are below par identify 50 or so key areas that are not always up to scratch; if compliance and paperwork is an issue – identify tasks that are not being done correctly; similarly identify management functions that fall short.

Now allocate each individual task a number.

Once a week randomly check five areas (I used to overwrite a couple of packs of cards with numbers, shuffle and get the chef himself to pick the five).

All five areas need to pass your with your approval for the chef to qualify for his bonus.

The randomness of the checking (a bit like the Lottery) means that all the jobs get done and you don't have the onerous task of checking 97 different things every week. It's also a bit of fun! Chefs tend to manage their teams better – particularly with the cleaning tasks!

Once they have qualified for the bonus the next criteria they need to meet is achieving a desired GP.

The table shows the incremental increase in GP for achieving higher margins.

With a starting point of 66% GP (the company average) each column represents the extra cash generated on food sales. For example on a weekly take of £7k net on food achieving a GP of 70% would generate another £350 (4% higher than the anticipated 66%)

This additional revenue can be shared as a cash bonus with Head Chef (and possibly Sous). The business takes 70% and chef takes 30% - £105 (£5,460) if he hits it all through the year.

The result?

Improved Head Chef performance or no bonus - the higher the GP achieved the higher the bonus.

All the necessary measuring and monitoring can be done easily from within the CaterCost System.

Kitchen cleaning tasks

(example)

1 Deep fat fryer oil
2 Under deep fat fryer
3 Stove hob
4 Stove oven
5 Under stove
6 Microwave 1 interior
7 Microwave 1 handle
8 Under and behind microwave 1
9
10
11
12
13
14
15
16
17
18
19
20
21
22
23
24
25
26
27
28
29
30

Compliance tasks

(example)

31 Fridge temperature sheets
32 Daily food probe records
33 Staff training
34 First aid box
35 Food storage areas
36 Chemical storage
37
38
39
40
41
42
43
44
45
46
47
48
49
50
51
52
53
54
55
56
57
58
59
60

Management tasks

(example)

61 Staff rotas complete
62 Stock count complete
63 Weekly specials board costing complete
64 Staff training given
65 Appraisals
66 Supplier updates
67 New menu creation
68
69
70
71
72
73
74
75
76
77
78
79
80
81
82
83
84
85
86
87
88
89
90

Chef incentive!

1. Set your minimum target GP
2. The table shows how much extra cash is made on your turnover by exceeding the target
   e.g. on a turnover of £4,500 and 3% above target GP an extra £135 is in the till
3. Incentivise your chef/kitchen team to hit healthy GPs by sharing this extra cash as a bonus

NET weekly food sales	Add 1% to GP	Add 2% to GP	Add 3% to GP	Add 4% to GP	Add 5% to GP	Add 6% to GP	Add 7% to GP	Add 8% to GP	Add 9% to GP
£4,000.00	£40.00	£80.00	£120.00	£160.00	£200.00	£240.00	£280.00	£320.00	£360.00
£4,250.00	£42.50	£85.00	£127.50	£170.00	£212.50	£255.00	£297.50	£340.00	£382.50
£4,500.00	£45.00	£90.00	£135.00	£180.00	£225.00	£270.00	£315.00	£360.00	£405.00
£4,750.00	£47.50	£95.00	£142.50	£190.00	£237.50	£285.00	£332.50	£380.00	£427.50
£5,000.00	£50.00	£100.00	£150.00	£200.00	£250.00	£300.00	£350.00	£400.00	£450.00
£5,250.00	£52.50	£105.00	£157.50	£210.00	£262.50	£315.00	£367.50	£420.00	£472.50
£5,500.00	£55.00	£110.00	£165.00	£220.00	£275.00	£330.00	£385.00	£440.00	£495.00
£5,750.00	£57.50	£115.00	£172.50	£230.00	£287.50	£345.00	£402.50	£460.00	£517.50
£6,000.00	£60.00	£120.00	£180.00	£240.00	£300.00	£360.00	£420.00	£480.00	£540.00
£6,250.00	£62.50	£125.00	£187.50	£250.00	£312.50	£375.00	£437.50	£500.00	£562.50
£6,500.00	£65.00	£130.00	£195.00	£260.00	£325.00	£390.00	£455.00	£520.00	£585.00
£6,750.00	£67.50	£135.00	£202.50	£270.00	£337.50	£405.00	£472.50	£540.00	£607.50
£7,000.00	£70.00	£140.00	£210.00	£280.00	£350.00	£420.00	£490.00	£560.00	£630.00
£7,250.00	£72.50	£145.00	£217.50	£290.00	£362.50	£435.00	£507.50	£580.00	£652.50
£7,500.00	£75.00	£150.00	£225.00	£300.00	£375.00	£450.00	£525.00	£600.00	£675.00
£7,750.00	£77.50	£155.00	£232.50	£310.00	£387.50	£465.00	£542.50	£620.00	£697.50
£8,000.00	£80.00	£160.00	£240.00	£320.00	£400.00	£480.00	£560.00	£640.00	£720.00
£8,250.00	£82.50	£165.00	£247.50	£330.00	£412.50	£495.00	£577.50	£660.00	£742.50
£8,500.00	£85.00	£170.00	£255.00	£340.00	£425.00	£510.00	£595.00	£680.00	£765.00
£8,750.00	£87.50	£175.00	£262.50	£350.00	£437.50	£525.00	£612.50	£700.00	£787.50
£9,000.00	£90.00	£180.00	£270.00	£360.00	£450.00	£540.00	£630.00	£720.00	£810.00
£9,250.00	£92.50	£185.00	£277.50	£370.00	£462.50	£555.00	£647.50	£740.00	£832.50
£9,500.00	£95.00	£190.00	£285.00	£380.00	£475.00	£570.00	£665.00	£760.00	£855.00
£9,750.00	£97.50	£195.00	£292.50	£390.00	£487.50	£585.00	£682.50	£780.00	£877.50
£10,000.00	£100.00	£200.00	£300.00	£400.00	£500.00	£600.00	£700.00	£800.00	£900.00

Our Team Rocks BASICS

Staff Member / Name	General Tasks for All Areas								Additional Tasks for Working the Bar							Additional Tasks for the Restaurant							Serving Drinks								Room Serve		Food Serve	
	Opening a shift	Closing a shift	Candles	Cutlery	Glasses	Sundays	Taking Payments	Gift Vouchers	Opening a shift extras	Closing a shift extras	Set up coffee station	EOD coffee station	Taking a food order	Sauce buckets	Cellar basics	Opening a shift extras	Closing a shift extras	Taking a drinks order	Taking a food order	Laying a perfect table	Setting up breakfast	Laying a breakfast table	Draught products	Wine in the BAR	Wine in the RESTAURANT	Tea for one/two	Coffee	De-caff coffee	Soft drinks and spirits	Licensing law	Room Service Breakfast	Room Service Dinner	Taking food to table	Basic food hygiene

We Rock! WOW!

Staff Member	Service with a Smile												Smooth Operator							Skills for the Future							Quals
	Meet and Greet	Goodbye	What's going on	Always know what to say	Magic Moments	Body Language	Gentle art of up-selling	"Yes I can" attitude	Service to make us smile	Customer complaints	Collecting customer info	The eating out experience	I know house wine	I know the wine list	I know starters	I know main courses	I know desserts	I know special products	I know refunds	Service profit chain	Organising Events	Marketing	Profit and Loss	Leadership & motivation	Supervisor	Manager	

209

27 Golden Rules

Golden Rule No 1
Focus on your numbers – you need to know your sales and costs every single day.

Golden Rule No 2
Decide what you want to earn - then use this to decide what size business (or businesses) you will need to operate to generate your desired income. It needs to be big enough to earn you a decent living/make you a fortune.'*

*delete as appropriate

Golden Rule No 3
You plan to be successful don't you? So ask yourself: 'Is it scalable? If your food is popular with customers and creates a big demand, will you outgrow your premises too soon? Relocation or expansion costs will quickly eat into your early profits.

Golden Rule 4
Without customers you have no business. Knowing your target customers inside out will give you a head start over your competition. In-depth customer analysis isn't rocket science – but not bothering to really match your offer to your target audience is bonkers.

Golden Rule No 5
Say to yourself: 'I am not my customer. Whatever my own personal feelings about food, I will provide the food my customers want to eat.'

Golden Rule No 6
Spend time on the boring stuff – costing your menu and setting the right margins for all the food you sell is VITAL and the lengths you go to will make or break your business.

Golden Rule No 7
Guessing food costs and profit margins is not an option. 'Food costing is an exact science.'

Golden Rule No 8
Your menu is a sales tool. Design your menu specifically to increase sales of your most profitable lines. It makes your customers happy, it makes your kitchen happy and it makes your bank manager happy. A triple whammy!

Golden Rule No 9
A brilliant and well balanced menu is central to your business. Use your imagination to create something fun and interesting for the customers and strategically profitable for you.

Golden Rule No 10
The devil is in the detail. Little tweaks to your food presentation translate into big differences in food profit and keep the Profit Vampires away.

Golden Rule No 11
Beware of Sod's Law – if anything can possibly go wrong with kitchen equipment it will and it will happen at a time designed to cause maximum inconvenience, difficulty and stress.

Golden Rule No 12
Customers want to know what's in their food. If you don't give them an option to select low calorie and allergen free menu items, you're effectively turning your back on a quarter of the UK's population.

Golden Rule No 13
Big menus suck! Doing one thing and doing it well is far better than doing a hundred things unexceptionally.

Golden Rule No 14
Be realistic – the size of your kitchen and the skill of your team will determine what you buy and prepare for your customers.

Golden Rule No 15
27g is 27g (not 29 or 25). Purchase a set of accurate scales and use them constantly.

Golden Rule No 16
Planning is everything – put in place a system to ensure you order and prepare the correct volumes of food.

Golden Rule No 17
Everyone advertises they do 'great food.' Don't be beige with your marketing – dare to be different and stand out from the crowd or your marketing efforts will be a complete waste of time and money.

Golden Rule No 18
Only lazy or incompetent restaurant owners don't create a database and measure the success of their marketing.

Golden Rule No 19
Cleanliness brings peace of mind. Although no one likes the paperwork, insist your team complies with the rules for food safety.

Golden Rule No 20
The dining experience goes way beyond the food. Pay attention to the detail of the environment you create for your guests.

Golden Rule No 21
You can't do it all on your own. Tell yourself: 'I need people around me who can do the stuff I can't; my job is to help them be the best they can be.'

Golden Rule No 22
Chefs can be weird – get over it!

Golden Rule No 23
The success or failure of your business is in the hands of people paid not much more than the minimum wage. Create a work culture and learning environment for your team with customer service at its core.

Golden Rule No 24
Accept that whatever happens in your business, good and bad, is down to you. Repeat this daily mantra: 'I can't run it successfully by ducking my responsibilities or by blaming anyone else...the buck stops with me.'

Golden Rule No 25
Managing your time effectively and prioritising tasks is central to the success or failure of your business.

Golden Rule No 26

Failures along the way are inevitable and will speed your journey to success. Tell yourself 'ultimate failure is not an option.' Adopt a positive mental approach even on the bad days. Think of Henry Ford's quote: 'Whether you think you can or think you can't – you're probably right.'

Golden Rule 27

Do a thousand little things absolutely the best you can, no detail is too small, work bloody hard at it and have a stack of fun along the way.

Acknowledgements

I owe a large debt to Tim, my loving, loyal and supportive partner who has backed me through every page, every re-write, every typo, and who has shown such enthusiasm to help me get the book off the ground.

To my daughters Katy and Zoe for never doubting their Mum and for mercifully skipping the hospitality gene.

To Clive, who was my husband and business partner through so many of the early learnings included in this book at The Ship, The Trout and the Bay View Inn.

To Andy, for professionally editing the content with buckets of encouragement, flair and sarky comments.

To Caroline and Sarah for getting me into the whole 'writing' thing and providing help and advice to get started (which is the hardest part believe me!)

To Jane for the layouts, design and countless amends

To Chris Adey, Dave Sargent, Si and Ben for being great chefs to work with and who have been constant inspirations for content.

Over the years I have worked with so many people in the hospitality industry – too many to thank individually for any input they may have had on my thinking in this book, but to all of them I am grateful for the gems, the learning the stories and the fun times.

Q&A

Alan Todd, Head of Catering Development, Punch Taverns
Clive Gayle, Chef de Partie, Radisson Blu Edwardian, London
Jamie Edwards, Executive Chef at Aqua Italia Restaurants
Ashley McCarthy, BII Licensee of the Year 2013, Chef/Proprietor Ye Old Sun Inn, Colton, Yorkshire
Allan Picket, Head Chef, Plateau, London
Gavin Austin, Head Chef, Oundle Mill, Northants
Adam Gray, Executive Chef, Skylon Restaurant, Royal Festival Hall
Andy Walsh, Catering Controller, Booker

What one thing do you wish you had known when you first started out as a chef/in hospitality?

AT – This is not a job, it's a way of life!

CG – I wish I had realised the value of getting a role in a big kitchen like Marco Pierre White's or Gordon Ramsay's

JE – How difficult it can be with so many different nationalities and personalities that you need to deal with or react to daily

AM – I wished I'd looked more into the future at the prospects an employer could offer and how that could have advanced me as an individual. Don't just look at the cash, look at the bigger picture, don't be blinkered. Within this industry you can easily work your way up the ladder – just make sure it's the right one and goes to the height you want

AP – The amount of time it would take to get where I am now

GA – The amount of sacrifice with regards to friends, time off, social events and broken promises

AG – How much hard work and sacrifice you have to make. It is relentless and even when you have a day off you are constantly thinking about all aspects of the kitchen, ordering, quality of food, service and staffing

AW – What a great opportunity I missed by going on holiday and not taking the job I was offered at Turnberry Hotel in Scotland. Also, don't take no for an answer – it's a fantastic industry with loads of great opportunities. You can work anywhere in the world if you wish

What is your Golden Rule for running a successful food operation?

AT – Keep your offer simple and do it really, really well!

CG – Be prepared for the quiet times when it's not so busy, never cut corners in the kitchen and be straight with your customers

JE – Always listen to your customers

AM – Be understanding and multi-functional. Know your weaknesses as well as your strengths. Set yourself targets that you don't believe you can achieve, then make yourself achieve them. Spread this work ethos throughout your team

AP – You need to have a proper understanding of costing, what your menu costs to make and what profit margin you are trying to achieve. If you cannot cost your menu you will fail in the long-term. Get someone you respect to teach you or put yourself on a course to learn how to do it

GA – Dealing with people conflicts and working as a team through communication

AG – Consistency in everything you do. Day-in, day-out, from food preparation, dish development and execution, customer service and satisfaction.
There are so many times when your experience going to a restaurant, pub or hotel where you have an enjoyable time, then you return later and the standards are not the same. Inconsistency loses you business

AW – Control your costs by better ordering, reducing wastage and portion control

Printed in Great Britain
by Amazon